Literary Taste:

How to Form it

Literary Taste:

How to Form it

*With Detailed Instructions for Collecting a
Complete Library of English Literature*

ARNOLD BENNETT

MANOR

Rockville, Maryland

2008

ISBN: 978-1-60450-346-3

Published by Arc Manor
P. O. Box 10339
Rockville, MD 20849-0339
www.ArcManor.com

Printed in the United States of America/United Kingdom

CONTENTS

1

THE AIM

At the beginning a misconception must be removed from the path. Many people, if not most, look on literary taste as an elegant accomplishment, by acquiring which they will complete themselves, and make themselves finally fit as members of a correct society. They are secretly ashamed of their ignorance of literature, in the same way as they would be ashamed of their ignorance of etiquette at a high entertainment, or of their inability to ride a horse if suddenly called upon to do so. There are certain things that a man ought to know, or to know about, and literature is one of them: such is their idea. They have learnt to dress themselves with propriety, and to behave with propriety on all occasions; they are fairly "up" in the questions of the day; by industry and enterprise they are succeeding in their vocations; it behoves them, then, not to forget that an acquaintance with literature is an indispensable part of a self-respecting man's personal baggage. Painting doesn't matter; music doesn't matter very much. But "everyone is supposed to know" about literature. Then, literature is such a charming distraction! Literary taste thus serves two purposes: as a certificate of correct culture and as a private pastime. A young professor of mathematics, immense at mathematics and games, dangerous at chess, capable of Haydn on the violin, once said to me, after listening to some chat on books, "Yes, I must take up literature." As though saying: "I was rather forgetting literature. However, I've polished off all these other things. I'll have a shy at literature now."

This attitude, or any attitude which resembles it, is wrong. To him who really comprehends what literature is, and what the function of literature is, this attitude is simply ludicrous. It is also fatal to the formation of literary taste. People who regard literary taste simply as an accomplishment, and literature simply as a distraction, will never truly succeed either in acquiring the accomplishment or in using it half-acquired as a distraction; though the one is the most perfect of distractions, and though the other is unsurpassed by any other accomplishment in elegance or in power to impress the universal snobbery of civilised mankind. Literature, instead of being an accessory, is the fundamental *sine qua non* of complete living. I am extremely anxious to avoid rhetorical exaggerations. I do not think I am guilty of one in asserting that he who has not been "presented to the freedom" of literature has not wakened up out of his prenatal sleep. He is merely not born. He can't see; he can't hear; he can't feel, in any full sense. He can only eat his dinner. What more than anything else annoys people who know the true function of literature, and have profited thereby, is the spectacle of so many thousands of individuals going about under the delusion that they are alive, when, as a fact, they are no nearer being alive than a bear in winter.

I will tell you what literature is! No—I only wish I could. But I can't. No one can. Gleams can be thrown on the secret, inklings given, but no more. I will try to give you an inkling. And, to do so, I will take you back into your own history, or forward into it. That evening when you went for a walk with your faithful friend, the friend from whom you hid nothing—or almost nothing ...! You were, in truth, somewhat inclined to hide from him the particular matter which monopolised your mind that evening, but somehow you contrived to get on to it, drawn by an overpowering fascination. And as your faithful friend was sympathetic and discreet, and flattered you by a respectful curiosity, you proceeded further and further into the said matter, growing more and more confidential, until at last you cried out, in a terrific whisper: "My boy, she is simply miraculous!" At that moment you were in the domain of literature.

Let me explain. Of course, in the ordinary acceptation of the word, she was not miraculous. Your faithful friend had never noticed that she was miraculous, nor had about forty thousand other fairly keen observers. She was just a girl. Troy had not been burnt for her. A girl cannot be called a miracle. If a girl is to be called a miracle, then you might call pretty nearly anything a miracle.... That is just it: you might. You can. You ought. Amid all the miracles of the universe you had just wakened up to one. You were full of your discovery. You were under a divine impulsion to impart that discovery. You had a strong sense of the marvellous beauty of something, and you had to share it. You were in a passion about something, and you had to vent yourself on somebody. You were drawn towards the whole of the rest of the human race. Mark the effect of your mood and utterance on your faithful friend. He knew that she was not a miracle. No other person could have made him believe that she was a miracle. But you, by the force and sincerity of your own vision of her, and by the fervour of your desire to make him participate in your vision, did for quite a long time cause him to feel that he had been blind to the miracle of that girl.

You were producing literature. You were alive. Your eyes were unlidded, your ears were unstopped, to some part of the beauty and the strangeness of the world; and a strong instinct within you forced you to tell someone. It was not enough for you that you saw and heard. Others had to see and hear. Others had to be wakened up. And they were! It is quite possible—I am not quite sure—that your faithful friend the very next day, or the next month, looked at some other girl, and suddenly saw that she, too, was miraculous! The influence of literature!

The makers of literature are those who have seen and felt the miraculous interestingness of the universe. And the greatest makers of literature are those whose vision has been the widest, and whose feeling has been the most intense. Your own fragment of insight was accidental, and perhaps temporary. *Their* lives are one long ecstasy of denying that the world is a dull place. Is it nothing to you to learn to understand that the world is not a dull place? Is it nothing to you to be led out of the tunnel on to the hillside, to have all your senses quickened, to be invigorated by the true savour of life, to feel your heart beating under that correct necktie of yours? These makers of literature render you their equals.

The aim of literary study is not to amuse the hours of leisure; it is to awake oneself, it is to be alive, to intensify one's capacity for pleasure, for sympathy, and for comprehension. It is not to affect one hour, but twenty-four hours. It is to change utterly one's relations with the world. An understanding appreciation of literature means an understanding appreciation of the world, and it means nothing else. Not isolated and unconnected parts of life, but all of life, brought together and correlated in a synthetic map! The spirit of literature is unifying; it joins the candle and the star, and by the magic of an image shows that the beauty of the greater is in the less. And, not content with the disclosure of beauty and the bringing together of all things whatever within its focus, it enforces a moral wisdom by the tracing everywhere of cause and effect. It consoles doubly—by the revelation of unsuspected loveliness, and by the proof that our lot is the common lot. It is the supreme cry of the discoverer, offering sympathy and asking for it in a single gesture. In attending a University Extension Lecture on the sources of Shakespeare's plots, or in studying the researches of George Saintsbury into the origins of English prosody, or in weighing the evidence for and against the assertion that Rousseau was a scoundrel, one is apt to forget what literature really is and is for. It is well to remind ourselves that literature is first and last a means of life, and that the enterprise of forming one's literary taste is an enterprise of learning how best to use this means of life. People who don't want to live, people who would sooner hibernate than feel intensely, will be wise to eschew literature. They had better, to quote from the finest passage in a fine poem, "sit around and eat blackberries." The sight of a "common bush afire with God" might upset their nerves.

2

YOUR PARTICULAR CASE

The attitude of the average decent person towards the classics of his own tongue is one of distrust— I had almost said, of fear. I will not take the case of Shakespeare, for Shakespeare is "taught" in schools; that is to say, the Board of Education and all authorities pedagogic bind themselves together in a determined effort to make every boy in the land a lifelong enemy of Shakespeare. (It is a mercy they don't "teach" Blake.) I will take, for an example, Sir Thomas Browne, as to whom the average person has no offensive juvenile memories. He is bound to have read somewhere that the style of Sir Thomas Browne is unsurpassed by anything in English literature. One day he sees the *Religio Medici* in a shop-window (or, rather, outside a shop-window, for he would hesitate about entering a bookshop), and he buys it, by way of a mild experiment. He does not expect to be enchanted by it; a profound instinct tells him that Sir Thomas Browne is "not in his line"; and in the result he is even less enchanted than he expected to be. He reads the introduction, and he glances at the first page or two of the work. He sees nothing but words. The work makes no appeal to him whatever. He is surrounded by trees, and cannot perceive the forest. He puts the book away. If Sir Thomas

Browne is mentioned, he will say, "Yes, very fine!" with a feeling of pride that he has at any rate bought and inspected Sir Thomas Browne. Deep in his heart is a suspicion that people who get enthusiastic about Sir Thomas Browne are vain and conceited *poseurs*. After a year or so, when he has recovered from the discouragement caused by Sir Thomas Browne, he may, if he is young and hopeful, repeat the experiment with Congreve or Addison. Same sequel! And so on for perhaps a decade, until his commerce with the classics finally expires! That, magazines and newish fiction apart, is the literary history of the average decent person.

And even your case, though you are genuinely preoccupied with thoughts of literature, bears certain disturbing resemblances to the drab case of the average person. You do not approach the classics with gusto—anyhow, not with the same gusto as you would approach a new novel by a modern author who had taken your fancy. You never murmured to yourself, when reading Gibbon's *Decline and Fall* in bed: "Well, I really must read one more chapter before I go to sleep!" Speaking generally, the classics do not afford you a pleasure commensurate with their renown. You peruse them with a sense of duty, a sense of doing the right thing, a sense of "improving yourself," rather than with a sense of gladness. You do not smack your lips; you say: "That is good for me." You make little plans for reading, and then you invent excuses for breaking the plans. Something new, something which is not a classic, will surely draw you away from a classic. It is all very well for you to pretend to agree with the verdict of the elect that *Clarissa Harlowe* is one of the greatest novels in the world—a new Kipling, or even a new number of a magazine, will cause you to neglect *Clarissa Harlowe,* just as though Kipling, etc., could not be kept for a few days without turning sour! So that you have to ordain rules for yourself, as: "I will not read anything else until I have read Richardson, or Gibbon, for an hour each day." Thus proving that you regard a classic as a pill, the swallowing of which merits jam! And the more modern a classic is, the more it resembles the stuff of the year and the less it resembles the classics of the centuries, the more easy and enticing do you find that classic. Hence you are glad that George Eliot, the Brontes, Thackeray, are considered as classics, because you really *do* enjoy them. Your sentiments concerning them approach your sentiments concerning a "rattling good story" in a magazine.

I may have exaggerated—or, on the other hand, I may have understated—the unsatisfactory characteristics of your particular case, but it is probable that in the mirror I hold up you recognise the rough outlines of your likeness. You do not care to admit it; but it is so. You are not content with yourself. The desire to be more truly literary persists in you. You feel that there is something wrong in you, but you cannot put your finger on the spot. Further, you feel that you are a bit of a sham. Something within you continually forces you to exhibit for the classics an enthusiasm which you do not sincerely feel. You even try to persuade yourself that you are enjoying a book, when the next moment you drop it in the middle and forget to resume it. You occasionally buy classical works, and do not read them at all; you practically decide that it is enough to possess them, and that the mere possession of them gives you a *cachet*. The truth is, you are a sham. And your soul is a sea of uneasy remorse. You reflect: "According to what Matthew Arnold says, I ought to be perfectly mad about Wordsworth's *Prelude*. And I am not. Why am I not? Have I got to be learned, to undertake a vast course of study, in order to be perfectly mad about Wordsworth's *Prelude?* Or am I born without the faculty of pure taste in literature, despite my vague longings? I do wish I could smack my lips over Wordsworth's *Prelude* as I did over that splendid story by H.G. Wells, *The Country of the Blind,* in the *Strand Magazine!*".... Yes, I am convinced that in your dissatisfied, your diviner moments, you address yourself in these terms. I am convinced that I have diagnosed your symptoms.

Now the enterprise of forming one's literary taste is an agreeable one; if it is not agreeable it cannot succeed. But this does not imply that it is an easy or a brief one. The enterprise of beating Colonel Bogey at golf is an agreeable one, but it means honest and regular work. A fact to be borne in mind always! You are certainly not going to realise your ambition—and so great, so influential an ambition!—by spasmodic and half-hearted effort. You must begin by making up your mind adequately. You must rise to the height of the affair. You must approach a grand undertaking in the grand manner. You ought to mark the day in the calendar as a solemnity. Human nature is weak, and has need of tricky aids, even in the pursuit of happiness. Time will be necessary to you, and time regularly and sacredly set apart. Many people affirm that they cannot be regular, that regularity numbs them. I think this is true of a very few people, and that in the rest the objection to regularity is merely an attempt to excuse idleness. I am inclined to think that you personally are capable of regularity. And I am sure that if you firmly and constantly devote certain specific hours on certain specific days of the week to this business of forming your literary taste, you will arrive at the goal much sooner. The simple act of resolution will help you. This is the first preliminary.

The second preliminary is to surround yourself with books, to create for yourself a bookish atmosphere.

The merely physical side of books is important—more important than it may seem to the inexperienced. Theoretically (save for works of reference), a student has need for but one book at a time. Theoretically, an amateur of literature might develop his taste by expending sixpence a week, or a penny a day, in one sixpenny edition of a classic after another sixpenny edition of a classic, and he might store his library in a hat-box or a biscuit-tin. But in practice he would have to be a monster of resolution to succeed in such conditions. The eye must be flattered; the hand must be flattered; the sense of owning must be flattered. Sacrifices must be made for the acquisition of literature. That which has cost a sacrifice is always endeared. A detailed scheme of buying books will come later, in the light of further knowledge. For the present, buy—buy whatever has received the *imprimatur* of critical authority. Buy without any immediate reference to what you will read. Buy! Surround yourself with volumes, as handsome as you can afford. And for reading, all that I will now particularly enjoin is a general and inclusive tasting, in order to attain a sort of familiarity with the look of "literature in all its branches." A turning over of the pages of a volume of Chambers's *Cyclopaedia of English Literature,* the third for preference, may be suggested as an admirable and a diverting exercise. You might mark the authors that flash an appeal to you.

3

WHY A CLASSIC IS A CLASSIC

The large majority of our fellow-citizens care as much about literature as they care about aeroplanes or the programme of the Legislature. They do not ignore it; they are not quite indifferent to it. But their interest in it is faint and perfunctory; or, if their interest happens to be violent, it is spasmodic. Ask the two hundred thousand persons whose enthusiasm made the vogue of a popular novel ten years ago what they think of that novel now, and you will gather that they have utterly forgotten it, and that they would no more dream of reading it again than of reading Bishop Stubbs's *Select Charters*. Probably if they did read it again they would not enjoy it—not because the said novel is a whit worse now than it was ten years ago; not because their taste has improved—but because they have not had sufficient practice to be able to rely on their taste as a means of permanent pleasure. They simply don't know from one day to the next what will please them.

In the face of this one may ask: Why does the great and universal fame of classical authors continue? The answer is that the fame of classical authors is entirely independent of the majority. Do you suppose that if

(why it continues)

17

thc famc of Shakespeare depended on the man in the street it would survive a fortnight? The fame of classical authors is originally made, and it is maintained, by a passionate few. Even whcn a first-class author has enjoyed immense success during his lifetime, the majority have never appreciated him so sincerely as they have appreciated second-rate men. He has always been reinforced by the ardour of the passionate few. And in the case of an author who has emerged into glory after his death the happy sequel has been due solely to the obstinate perseverance of the few. They could not leave him alone; they would not. They kept on savouring him, and talking about him, and buying him, and they generally behaved with such eager zeal, and they were so authoritative and sure of themselves, that at last the majority grew accustomed to the sound of his name and placidly agreed to the proposition that he was a genius; the majority really did not care very much either way.

And it is by the passionate few that the renown of genius is kept alive from one generation to another. These few are always at work. They are always rediscovering genius. Their curiosity and enthusiasm are exhaustless, so that there is little chance of genius being ignored. And, moreover, they are always working either for or against the verdicts of the majority. The majority can make a reputation, but it is too careless to maintain it. If, by accident, the passionate few agree with the majority in a particular instance, they will frequently remind the majority that such and such a reputation has been made, and the majority will idly concur: "Ah, yes. By the way, we must not forget that such and such a reputation exists." Without that persistent memory-jogging the reputation would quickly fall into the oblivion which is death. The passionate few only have their way by reason of the fact that they are genuinely interested in literature, that literature matters to them. They conquer by their obstinacy alone, by their eternal repetition of the same statements. Do you suppose they could prove to the man in the street that Shakespeare was a great artist? The said man would not even understand the terms they employed. But when he is told ten thousand times, and generation after generation, that Shakespeare was a great artist, the said man believes—not by reason, but by faith. And he too repeats that Shakespeare was a great artist, and he buys the complete works of Shakespeare and puts them on his shelves, and he goes to see the marvellous stage-effects which accompany *King Lear* or *Hamlet,* and comes back religiously convinced that Shakespeare was a great artist. All because the passionate few could not keep their admiration of Shakespeare to themselves. This is not cynicism; but truth. And it is important that those who wish to form their literary taste should grasp it.

What causes the passionate few to make such a fuss about literature? There can be only one reply. They find a keen and lasting pleasure in literature. They enjoy literature as some men enjoy beer. The recurrence of this pleasure naturally keeps their interest in literature very much alive. They are for ever making new researches, for ever practising on themselves. They learn to understand themselves. They learn to know what they want. Their taste becomes surer and surer as their experience lengthens. They do not enjoy to-day what will seem tedious to them to-morrow. When they find a book tedious, no amount of popular clatter will persuade them that it is pleasurable; and when they find it pleasurable no chill silence of the street-crowds will affect their conviction that the book is good and permanent. They have faith in themselves. What are the

qualities in a book which give keen and lasting pleasure to the passionate few? This is a question so difficult that it has never yet been completely answered.
You may talk lightly about truth, insight, knowledge,
wisdom, humour, and beauty. But these comfortable
words do not really carry you very far, for each of them
has to be defined, especially the first and last. It is all
very well for Keats in his airy manner to assert that
beauty is truth, truth beauty, and that that is all he
knows or needs to know. I, for one, need to know a lot
more. And I never shall know. Nobody, not even Hazlitt nor Sainte-Beuve, has ever finally explained why
he thought a book beautiful. I take the first fine lines
that come to hand—

> *The woods of Arcady are dead,*
> *And over is their antique joy—*

and I say that those lines are beautiful, because they
give me pleasure. But why? No answer! I only know
that the passionate few will, broadly, agree with me in
deriving this mysterious pleasure from those lines. I
am only convinced that the liveliness of our pleasure
in those and many other lines by the same author will
ultimately cause the majority to believe, by faith, that
W.B. Yeats is a genius. The one reassuring aspect of
the literary affair is that the passionate few are passionate about the same things. A continuance of interest does, in actual practice, lead ultimately to the
same judgments. There is only the difference in width
of interest. Some of the passionate few lack catholic-
ity, or, rather, the whole of their interest is confined to
one narrow channel; they have none left over. These
men help specially to vitalise the reputations of the
narrower geniuses: such as Crashaw. But their active
predilections never contradict the general verdict of
the passionate few; rather they reinforce it.

A classic is a work which gives pleasure to the minority which is intensely and permanently interested in literature. It lives on because the minority, eager to renew the sensation of pleasure, is eternally curious and is therefore engaged in an eternal process of re-discovery. A classic does not survive for any ethical reason. It does not survive because it conforms to certain canons, or because neglect would not kill it. It survives because it is a source of pleasure, and be-cause the passionate few can no more neglect it than a bee can neglect a flower. The passionate few do not read "the right things" because they are right. That is to put the cart before the horse. "The right things" are the right things solely because the passionate few *like* reading them. Hence—and I now arrive at my point—the one primary essential to literary taste is a hot in-terest in literature. If you have that, all the rest will come. It matters nothing that at present you fail to find pleasure in certain classics. The driving impulse of your interest will force you to acquire experience, and experience will teach you the use of the means of pleasure. You do not know the secret ways of yourself: that is all. A continuance of interest must inevitably bring you to the keenest joys. But, of course, experi-ence may be acquired judiciously or injudiciously, just as Putney may be reached *via* Walham Green or *via* St. Petersburg.

4

WHERE TO BEGIN

I wish particularly that my readers should not be intimidated by the apparent vastness and complexity of this enterprise of forming the literary taste. It is not so vast nor so complex as it looks. There is no need whatever for the inexperienced enthusiast to confuse and frighten himself with thoughts of "literature in all its branches." Experts and pedagogues (chiefly pedagogues) have, for the purpose of convenience, split literature up into divisions and sub-divisions—such as prose and poetry; or imaginative, philosophic, historical; or elegiac, heroic, lyric; or religious and profane, etc., *ad infinitum*. But the greater truth is that literature is all one—and indivisible. The idea of the unity of literature should be well planted and fostered in the head. All literature is the expression of feeling, of passion, of emotion, caused by a sensation of the interestingness of life. What drives a historian to write history? Nothing but the overwhelming impression made upon him by the survey of past times. He is forced into an attempt to reconstitute the picture for others. If hitherto you have failed to perceive that a historian is a being in strong emotion, trying to convey his emotion to others, read the passage in the *Memoirs* of Gibbon, in which he describes how he finished the *Decline and Fall*. You will probably never again look upon the *Decline and Fall* as a "dry" work.

What applies to history applies to the other "dry" branches. Even Johnson's Dictionary is packed with emotion. Read the last paragraph of the preface to it: "In this work, when it shall be found that much is omitted, let it not be forgotten that much likewise is performed.... It may repress the triumph of malignant criticism to observe that if our language is not here fully displayed, I have only failed in an attempt which no human powers have hitherto completed...." And so on to the close: "I have protracted my work till most of those whom I wish to please have sunk into the grave, and success and miscarriage are empty sounds: I therefore dismiss it with frigid tranquillity, having little to fear or hope from censure or from praise." Yes, tranquillity; but not frigid! The whole passage, one of the finest in English prose, is marked by the heat of emotion. You may discover the same quality in such books as Spencer's *First Principles*. You may discover it everywhere in literature, from the cold fire of Pope's irony to the blasting temperatures of Swinburne. Literature does not begin till emotion has begun.

There is even no essential, definable difference between those two great branches, prose and poetry. For prose may have rhythm. All that can be said is that verse will scan, while prose will not. The difference is purely formal. Very few poets have succeeded in being so poetical as Isaiah, Sir Thomas Browne, and Ruskin have been in prose. It can only be stated that, as a rule, writers have shown an instinctive tendency to choose verse for the expression of the very highest emotion. The supreme literature is in verse, but the finest achievements in prose approach so nearly to the

23

fincst achievements in verse that it is ill work decid-
ing between them. In the sense in which poetry is best
understood, all literature is poetry—or is, at any rate,
poetical in quality. Macaulay's ill-informed and unjust
denunciations live because his genuine emotion made
them into poetry, while his *Lays of Ancient Rome* are
dead because they are not the expression of a genuine
emotion. As the literary taste develops, this quality of
emotion, restrained or loosed, will be more and more
widely perceived at large in literature. It is the quality
that must be looked for. It is the quality that unifies
literature (and all the arts).

It is not merely useless, it is harmful, for you to map
out literature into divisions and branches, with different laws, rules, or canons. The first thing is to obtain
some possession of literature. When you have actually felt some of the emotion which great writers have
striven to impart to you, and when your emotions
become so numerous and puzzling that you feel the
need of arranging them and calling them by names,
then—and not before—you can begin to study what
has been attempted in the way of classifying and tick-
eting literature. Manuals and treatises are excellent
things in their kind, but they are simply dead weight
at the start. You can only acquire really useful general ideas by first acquiring particular ideas, and put-
ting those particular ideas together. You cannot make
bricks without straw. Do not worry about literature
in the abstract, about theories as to literature. Get at
it. Get hold of literature in the concrete as a dog gets
hold of a bone. If you ask me where you ought to begin, I shall gaze at you as I might gaze at the faithful
animal if he inquired which end of the bone he ought
to attack. It doesn't matter in the slightest degree
where you begin. Begin wherever the fancy takes you
to begin. Literature is a whole.

There is only one restriction for you. You must begin with an acknowledged classic; you must eschew modern works. The reason for this does not imply any depreciation of the present age at the expense of past ages. Indeed, it is important, if you wish ultimately to have a wide, catholic taste, to guard against the too common assumption that nothing modern will stand comparison with the classics. In every age there have been people to sigh: "Ah, yes. Fifty years ago we had a few great writers. But they are all dead, and no young ones are arising to take their place." This attitude of mind is deplorable, if not silly, and is a certain proof of narrow taste. It is a surety that in 1959 gloomy and egregious persons will be saying: "Ah, yes. At the beginning of the century there were great poets like Swinburne, Meredith, Francis Thompson, and Yeats. Great novelists like Hardy and Conrad. Great historians like Stubbs and Maitland, etc., etc. But they are all dead now, and whom have we to take their place?" It is not until an age has receded into history, and all its mediocrity has dropped away from it, that we can see it as it is—as a group of men of genius. We forget the immense amount of twaddle that the great epochs produced. The total amount of fine literature created in a given period of time differs from epoch to epoch, but it does not differ much. And we may be perfectly sure that our own age will make a favourable impression upon that excellent judge, posterity. Therefore, beware of disparaging the present in your own mind. While temporarily ignoring it, dwell upon the idea that its chaff contains about as much wheat as any similar quantity of chaff has contained wheat.

The reason why you must avoid modern works at the beginning is simply that you are not in a position to choose among modern works. Nobody at all is quite in a position to choose with certainty among modern works. To sift the wheat from the chaff is a process that takes an exceedingly long time. Modern works have to pass before the bar of the taste of successive generations. Whereas, with classics, which have been through the ordeal, almost the reverse is the case. *Your taste has to pass before the bar of the classics.* That is the point. If you differ with a classic, it is you who are wrong, and not the book. If you differ with a modern work, you may be wrong or you may be right, but no judge is authoritative enough to decide. Your taste is unformed. It needs guidance, and it needs authoritative guidance. Into the business of forming literary taste faith enters. You probably will not specially care for a particular classic at first. If you did care for it at first, your taste, so far as that classic is concerned, would be formed, and our hypothesis is that your taste is not formed. How are you to arrive at the stage of caring for it? Chiefly, of course, by examining it and honestly trying to understand it. But this process is materially helped by an act of faith, by the frame of mind which says: "I know on the highest authority that this thing is fine, that it is capable of giving me pleasure. Hence I am determined to find pleasure in it." Believe me that faith counts enormously in the development of that wide taste which is the instrument of wide pleasures. But it must be faith founded on unassailable authority.

5

HOW TO READ A CLASSIC

Let us begin experimental reading with Charles Lamb. I choose Lamb for various reasons: He is a great writer, wide in his appeal, of a highly sympathetic temperament; and his finest achievements are simple and very short. Moreover, he may usefully lead to other and more complex matters, as will appear later. Now, your natural tendency will be to think of Charles Lamb as a book, because he has arrived at the stage of being a classic. Charles Lamb was a man, not a book. It is extremely important that the beginner in literary study should always form an idea of the man behind the book. The book is nothing but the expression of the man. The book is nothing but the man trying to talk to you, trying to impart to you some of his feelings. An experienced student will divine the man from the book, will understand the man by the book, as is, of course, logically proper. But the beginner will do well to aid himself in understanding the book by means of independent information about the man. He will thus at once relate the book to something human, and strengthen in his mind the essential notion of the connection between literature and life. The earliest literature was delivered orally direct by the artist to the recipient. In some respects this arrangement was ideal.

Changes in the constitution of society have rendered it impossible. Nevertheless, we can still, by the exercise of the imagination, hear mentally the accents of the artist speaking to us. We must so exercise our imagination as to feel the man behind the book.

Some biographical information about Lamb should be acquired. There are excellent short biographies of him by Canon Ainger in the *Dictionary of National Biography,* in Chambers's *Encyclopaedia,* and in Chambers's *Cyclopaedia of English Literature.* If you have none of these (but you ought to have the last), there are Mr. E.V. Lucas's exhaustive *Life* (Methuen, 7s. 6d.), and, cheaper, Mr. Walter Jerrold's *Lamb* (Bell and Sons, 1s.); also introductory studies prefixed to various editions of Lamb's works. Indeed, the facilities for collecting materials for a picture of Charles Lamb as a human being are prodigious. When you have made for yourself such a picture, read the *Essays of Elia* the light of it. I will choose one of the most celebrated, *Dream Children: A Reverie.* At this point, kindly put my book down, and read *Dream Children.* Do not say to yourself that you will read it later, but read it now. When you have read it, you may proceed to my next paragraph.

You are to consider *Dream Children* as a human document. Lamb was nearing fifty when he wrote it. You can see, especially from the last line, that the death of his elder brother, John Lamb, was fresh and heavy on his mind. You will recollect that in youth he had had a disappointing love-affair with a girl named Ann Simmons, who afterwards married a man named Bartrum. You will know that one of the influences of his childhood was his grandmother Field, housekeeper of Blakesware House, in Hertfordshire, at which mansion he sometimes spent his holidays. You will know that he was a bachelor, living with his sister Mary, who was subject to homicidal mania. And you will see in this essay, primarily, a supreme expression of the increasing loneliness of his life. He constructed all that preliminary tableau of paternal pleasure in order to bring home to you in the most poignant way his feeling of the solitude of his existence, his sense of all that he had missed and lost in the world. The key of the essay is one of profound sadness. But note that he makes his sadness beautiful; or, rather, he shows the beauty that resides in sadness. You watch him sitting there in his "bachelor arm-chair," and you say to yourself: "Yes, it was sad, but it was somehow beautiful." When you have said that to yourself, Charles Lamb, so far as you are concerned, has accomplished his chief aim in writing the essay. How exactly he produces his effect can never be fully explained. But one reason of his success is certainly his regard for truth. He does not falsely idealise his brother, nor the relations between them. He does not say, as a sentimentalist would have said, "Not the slightest cloud ever darkened our relations;" nor does he exaggerate his solitude. Being a sane man, he has too much common-sense to assemble all his woes at once. He might have told you that Bridget was a homicidal maniac; what he does tell you is that she was faithful. Another reason of his success is his continual regard for beautiful things and fine actions, as illustrated in the major characteristics of his grandmother and his brother, and in the detailed description of Blakesware House and the gardens thereof.

Then, subordinate to the main purpose, part of the machinery of the main purpose, is the picture of the children—real children until the moment when they fade away. The traits of childhood are accurately and humorously put in again and again: "Here John smiled, as much as to say, 'That would be foolish indeed.'" "Here little Alice spread her hands." "Here Alice's little right foot playcd an involuntary movement, till, upon my looking grave, it desisted." "Here John expanded all his eyebrows, and tried to look couragcous." "Here John slily deposited back upon the plate a bunch of grapes." "Here the children fell a-crying ... and prayed me to tell them some stories about their pretty dead mother." And the exquisite: "Here Alice put out one of her dear mother's looks, too tender to be upbraiding." Incidentally, while preparing his ultimate solemn effect, Lamb has inspired you with a new, intensified vision of the wistful beauty of children—their imitativeness, their facile and generous emotions, their anxiety to be correct, their ingenuous haste to escape from grief into joy. You can see these children almost as clearly and as tenderly as Lamb saw them. For days afterwards you will not be able to look upon a child without recalling Lamb's portrayal of the grace of childhood. He will have shared with you his perception of beauty. If you possess children, he will have renewed for you the charm which custom does very decidedly stale. It is further to be noticed that the measure of his success in picturing the children is the measure of his success in his main effect. The more real they seem, the more touching is the revelation of the fact that they do not exist, and never have existed. And if you were moved by the reference to their "pretty dead mother," you will be still more moved when you learn that the girl who would have been their mother is not dead and is not Lamb's.

As, having read the essay, you reflect upon it, you will see how its emotional power over you has sprung from the sincere and unexaggerated expression of actual emotions exactly remembered by someone who had an eye always open for beauty, who was, indeed, obsessed by beauty. The beauty of old houses and gardens and aged virtuous characters, the beauty

of children, the beauty of companionships, the soft-
ening beauty of dreams in an arm-chair—all these
are brought together and mingled with the grief and
regret which were the origin of the mood. Why is
Dream Children a classic? It is a classic because it
transmits to you, as to generations before you, distinguished emotion, because it makes you respond
to the throb of life more intensely, more justly, and
more nobly. And it is capable of doing this because
Charles Lamb had a very distinguished, a very sen-
sitive, and a very honest mind. His emotions were
noble. He felt so keenly that he was obliged to find
relief in imparting his emotions. And his mental pro-
cesses were so sincere that he could neither exaggerate nor diminish the truth. If he had lacked any one
of these three qualities, his appeal would have been
narrowed and weakened, and he would not have become a classic. Either his feelings would have been
deficient in supreme beauty, and therefore less wor-
thy to be imparted, or he would not have had sufficient force to impart them; or his honesty would not
have been equal to the strain of imparting them accurately. In any case, he would not have set up in you
that vibration which we call pleasure, and which is
super-eminently caused by vitalising participation
in high emotion. As Lamb sat in his bachelor arm-
chair, with his brother in the grave, and the faithful
homicidal maniac by his side, he really did think to
himself, "This is beautiful. Sorrow is beautiful. Disappointment is beautiful. Life is beautiful. *I must
tell them*. I must make them understand." Because
he still makes you understand he is a classic. And
now I seem to hear you say, "But what about Lamb's
famous literary style? Where does that come in?"

6

THE QUESTION OF STYLE

In discussing the value of particular books, I have heard people say—people who were timid about expressing their views of literature in the presence of literary men: "It may be bad from a literary point of view, but there are very good things in it." Or: "I dare say the style is very bad, but really the book is very interesting and suggestive." Or: "I'm not an expert, and so I never bother my head about good style. All I ask for is good matter. And when I have got it, critics may say what they like about the book." And many other similar remarks, all showing that in the minds of the speakers there existed a notion that style is something supplementary to, and distinguishable from, matter; a sort of notion that a writer who wanted to be classical had first to find and arrange his matter, and then dress it up elegantly in a costume of style, in order to please beings called literary critics.

This is a misapprehension. Style cannot be distinguished from matter. When a writer conceives an idea he conceives it in a form of words. That form of words constitutes his style, and it is absolutely governed by the idea. The idea can only exist in words, and it can only exist in one form of words. You cannot say exactly the same thing in two different ways. Slightly alter the expression, and you slightly alter the idea. Surely it is obvious that the expression cannot be altered without altering the thing expressed! A writer, having conceived and expressed an idea, may, and probably will, "polish it up." But what does he polish up? To say that he polishes up his style is merely to say that he is polishing up his idea, that he has discovered faults or imperfections in his idea, and is perfecting it. An idea exists in proportion as it is expressed; it exists when it is expressed, and not before. It expresses itself. A clear idea is expressed clearly, and a vague idea vaguely. You need but take your own case and your own speech. For just as science is the development of common-sense, so is literature the development of common daily speech. The difference between science and common-sense is simply one of degree; similarly with speech and literature. Well, when you "know what you think," you succeed in saying what you think, in making yourself understood. When you "don't know what to think," your expressive tongue halts. And note how in daily life the characteristics of your style follow your mood; how tender it is when you are tender, how violent when you are violent. You have said to yourself in moments of emotion: "If only I could write—," etc. You were wrong. You ought to have said: "If only I could *think*—on this high plane." When you have thought clearly you have never had any difficulty in saying what you thought, though you may occasionally have had some difficulty in keeping it to yourself. And when you cannot express yourself, depend upon it that you have nothing precise to express, and that what incommodes you is not the vain desire to express, but the vain desire to *think* more clearly. All this just to illustrate how style and matter are co-existent, and inseparable, and alike.

You cannot have good matter with bad style. Examine the point more closely. A man wishes to convey a fine idea to you. He employs a form of words. That form of words is his style. Having read, you say: "Yes, this idea is fine." The writer has therefore achieved his end. But in what imaginable circumstances can you say: "Yes, this idea is fine, but the style is not fine"? The sole medium of communication between you and the author has been the form of words. The fine idea has reached you. How? In the words, by the words. Hence the fineness must be in the words. You may say, superiorly: "He has expressed himself clumsily, but I can *see* what he means." By what light? By something in the words, in the style. That something is fine. Moreover, if the style is clumsy, are you sure that you can see what he means? You cannot be quite sure. And at any rate, you cannot see distinctly. The "matter" is what actually reaches you, and it must necessarily be affected by the style.

Still further to comprehend what style is, let me ask you to think of a writer's style exactly as you would think of the gestures and manners of an acquaintance. You know the man whose demeanour is "always calm," but whose passions are strong. How do you know that his passions are strong? Because he "gives them away" by some small, but important, part of his demeanour, such as the twitching of a lip or the whitening of the knuckles caused by clenching the hand. In other words, his demeanour, fundamentally, is not calm. You know the man who is always "smoothly polite and agreeable," but who affects you unpleasantly. Why does he affect you unpleasantly? Because he is tedious, and therefore disagreeable, and because his politeness is not real politeness. You know the man who is awkward, shy, clumsy, but who, nevertheless, impresses you with a sense of dignity and force. Why? Because mingled with that awkwardness and so forth *is* dignity. You know the blunt, rough fellow whom you instinctively guess to be affectionate—because there is "something in his tone" or "something in his eyes." In every instance the demeanour, while perhaps seeming to be contrary to the character, is really in accord with it. The demeanour never contradicts the character. It is one part of the character that contradicts another part of the character. For, after all, the blunt man *is* blunt, and the awkward man *is* awkward, and these characteristics are defects. The demeanour merely expresses them. The two men would be better if, while conserving their good qualities, they had the superficial attributes of smoothness and agreeableness possessed by the gentleman who is unpleasant to you. And as regards this latter, it is not his superficial attributes which are unpleasant to you; but his other qualities. In the end the character is shown in the demeanour; and the demeanour is a consequence of the character and resembles the character. So with style and matter. You may argue that the blunt, rough man's demeanour is unfair to his tenderness. I do not think so. For his churlishness is really very trying and painful, even to the man's wife, though a moment's tenderness will make her and you forget it. The man really is churlish, and much more often than he is tender. His demeanour is merely just to his character. So, when a writer annoys you for ten pages and then enchants you for ten lines, you must not explode against his style. You must not say that his style won't let his matter "come out." You must remember the churlish, tender man. The more you reflect, the more clearly you will see that faults and excellences of style are faults and excellences of matter itself.

One of the most striking illustrations of this neglected truth is Thomas Carlyle. How often has it been said that Carlyle's matter is marred by the harshness and the eccentricities of his style? But Carlyle's matter is harsh and eccentric to precisely the same degree as his style is harsh and eccentric. Carlyle was harsh and eccentric. His behaviour was frequently ridiculous, if it were not abominable. His judgments were often extremely bizarre. When you read one of Carlyle's fierce diatribes, you say to yourself: "This is splendid. The man's enthusiasm for justice and truth is glorious." But you also say: "He is a little unjust and a little untruthful. He goes too far. He lashes too hard." These things are not the style; they are the matter. And when, as in his greatest moments, he is emotional and restrained at once, you say: "This is the real Carlyle." Kindly notice how perfect the style has become! No harshnesses or eccentricities now! And if that particular matter is the "real" Carlyle, then that particular style is Carlyle's "real" style. But when you say "real" you would more properly say "best." "This is the best Carlyle." If Carlyle had always been at his best he would have counted among the supreme geniuses of the world. But he was a mixture. His style is the expression of the mixture. The faults are only in the style because they are in the matter.

You will find that, in classical literature, the style always follows the mood of the matter. Thus, Charles Lamb's essay on *Dream Children* begins quite simply, in a calm, narrative manner, enlivened by a certain quippishness concerning the children. The style is grave when great-grandmother Field is the subject, and when the author passes to a rather elaborate impression of the picturesque old mansion it becomes as it were consciously beautiful. This beauty is intensified in the description of the still more beautiful garden. But the real dividing point of the essay occurs when Lamb approaches his elder brother. He unmistakably marks the point with the phrase: *"Then, in*

THE QUESTION OF STYLE

somewhat a more heightened tone, I told how," etc.
Henceforward the style increases in fervour and in solemnity until the culmination of the essay is reached:
"And while I stood gazing, both the children gradually grew fainter to my view, receding and still receding till nothing at last but two mournful features
were seen in the uttermost distance, which, without
speech, strangely impressed upon me the effects of
speech...." Throughout, the style is governed by the
matter. "Well," you say, "of course it is. It couldn't be
otherwise. If it were otherwise it would be ridiculous.
A man who made love as though he were preaching a
sermon, or a man who preached a sermon as though
he were teasing schoolboys, or a man who described
a death as though he were describing a practical joke,
must necessarily be either an ass or a lunatic." Just so.
You have put it in a nutshell. You have disposed of the
problem of style so far as it can be disposed of.

But what do those people mean who say: "I read such
and such an author for the beauty of his style alone"?
Personally, I do not clearly know what they mean (and
I have never been able to get them to explain), unless
they mean that they read for the beauty of sound alone.
When you read a book there are only three things of
which you may be conscious: (1) The significance of the
words, which is inseparably bound up with the thought.
(2) The look of the printed words on the page—I do not
suppose that anybody reads any author for the visual
beauty of the words on the page. (3) The sound of the
words, either actually uttered or imagined by the brain
to be uttered. Now it is indubitable that words differ in
beauty of sound. To my mind one of the most beautiful
words in the English language is "pavement." Enunci-
ate it, study its sound, and see what you think. It is also
indubitable that certain combinations of words have
a more beautiful sound than certain other combina-

tions. Thus Tennyson held that the most beautiful line he ever wrote was:

The mellow ouzel fluting in the elm.

Perhaps, as sound, it was. Assuredly it makes a beautiful succession of sounds, and recalls the bird-sounds which it is intended to describe. But does it live in the memory as one of the rare great Tennysonian lines? It does not. It has charm, but the charm is merely curious or pretty. A whole poem composed of lines with no better recommendation than that line has would remain merely curious or pretty. It would not permanently interest. It would be as insipid as a pretty woman who had nothing behind her prettiness. It would not live. One may remark in this connection how the merely verbal felicities of Tennyson have lost our esteem. Who will now proclaim the *Idylls of the King* as a masterpiece? Of the thousands of lines written by him which please the ear, only those survive of which the matter is charged with emotion. No! As regards the man who professes to read an author "for his style alone," I am inclined to think either that he will soon get sick of that author, or that he is deceiving himself and means the author's general temperament—not the author's verbal style, but a peculiar quality which runs through all the matter written by the author. Just as one may like a man for something which is always coming out of him, which one cannot define, and which is of the very essence of the man.

In judging the style of an author, you must employ the same canons as you use in judging men. If you do this you will not be tempted to attach importance to trifles that are negligible. There can be no lasting friendship without respect. If an author's style is such that you cannot *respect* it, then you may be sure that, despite any present pleasure which you may obtain from that author, there is something wrong with his matter, and that the pleasure will soon cloy. You must examine your sentiments towards an author. If when you have read an author you are pleased, without being conscious of aught but his mellifluousness, just conceive what your feelings would be after spending a month's holiday with a merely mellifluous man. If an author's style has pleased you, but done nothing except make you giggle, then reflect upon the ultimate tediousness of the man who can do nothing but jest. On the other hand, if you are impressed by what an author has said to you, but are aware of verbal clumsinesses in his work, you need worry about his "bad style" exactly as much and exactly as little as you would worry about the manners of a kindhearted, keen-brained friend who was dangerous to carpets with a tea-cup in his hand. The friend's antics in a drawing-room are somewhat regrettable, but you would not say of him that his manners were bad. Again, if an author's style dazzles you instantly and blinds you to everything except its brilliant self, ask your soul, before you begin to admire his matter, what would be your final opinion of a man who at the first meeting fired his personality into you like a broadside. Reflect that, as a rule, the people whom you have come to esteem communicated themselves to you gradually, that they did not begin the entertainment with fireworks. In short, look at literature as you would look at life, and you cannot fail to perceive that, essentially, the style is the man. Decidedly you will never assert that you care nothing for style, that your enjoyment of an author's matter is unaffected by his style. And you will never assert, either, that style alone suffices for you.

If you are undecided upon a question of style, whether leaning to the favourable or to the unfavourable, the most prudent course is to forget that literary style ex-

ists. For, indeed, as style is understood by most people
who have not analysed their impressions under the
influence of literature, there *is* no such thing as literary style. You cannot divide literature into two ele-
ments and say: This is matter and that style. Further,
the significance and the worth of literature are to be
comprehended and assessed in the same way as the
significance and the worth of any other phenomenon:
by the exercise of common-sense. Common-sense will
tell you that nobody, not even a genius, can be simul-
taneously vulgar and distinguished, or beautiful and
ugly, or precise and vague, or tender and harsh. And
common-sense will therefore tell you that to try to set
up vital contradictions between matter and style is ab-
surd. When there is a superficial contradiction, one of
the two mutually-contradicting qualities is of far less
importance than the other. If you refer literature to the
standards of life, common-sense will at once decide
which quality should count heaviest in your esteem.
You will be in no danger of weighing a mere maladroit-
ness of manner against a fine trait of character, or of
letting a graceful deportment blind you to a fundamental vacuity. When in doubt, ignore style, and think
of the matter as you would think of an individual.

7

WRESTLING WITH AN AUTHOR

Having disposed, so far as is possible and necessary, of that formidable question of style, let us now return to Charles Lamb, whose essay on *Dream Children* was the originating cause of our inquiry into style. As we have made a beginning of Lamb, it will be well to make an end of him. In the preliminary stages of literary culture, nothing is more helpful, in the way of kindling an interest and keeping it well alight, than to specialise for a time on one author, and particularly on an author so frankly and curiously "human" as Lamb is. I do not mean that you should imprison yourself with Lamb's complete works for three months, and read nothing else. I mean that you should regularly devote a proportion of your learned leisure to the study of Lamb until you are acquainted with all that is important in his work and about his work. (You may buy the complete works in prose and verse of Charles and Mary Lamb, edited by that unsurpassed expert Mr. Thomas Hutchison, and published by the Oxford University Press, in two volumes for four shillings the pair!) There is no reason why you should not become a modest specialist in Lamb. He is the very man for you; neither voluminous, nor difficult, nor uncomfortably lofty; always

either amusing or touching; and—most important—
himself passionately addicted to literature. You cannot like Lamb without liking literature in general.
And you cannot read Lamb without learning about
literature in general; for books were his hobby, and
he was a critic of the first rank. His letters are full of
literariness. You will naturally read his letters; you
should not only be infinitely diverted by them (there
are no better epistles), but you should receive from
them much light on the works.

It is a course of study that I am suggesting to you. It
means a certain amount of sustained effort. It means
slightly more resolution, more pertinacity, and more
expenditure of brain-tissue than are required for
reading a newspaper. It means, in fact, "work." Perhaps you did not bargain for work when you joined
me. But I do not think that the literary taste can be
satisfactorily formed unless one is prepared to put
one's back into the affair. And I may prophesy to
you, by way of encouragement, that, in addition to
the advantages of familiarity with masterpieces, of
increased literary knowledge, and of a wide introduction to the true bookish atmosphere and "feel" of
things, which you will derive from a comprehensive
study of Charles Lamb, you will also be conscious
of a moral advantage—the very important and very
inspiring advantage of really "knowing something
about something." You will have achieved a definite
step; you will be proudly aware that you have put
yourself in a position to judge as an expert whatever you may hear or read in the future concerning
Charles Lamb. This legitimate pride and sense of accomplishment will stimulate you to go on further;
it will generate steam. I consider that this indirect
moral advantage even outweighs, for the moment,
the direct literary advantages.

Now, I shall not shut my eyes to a possible result of your diligent intercourse with Charles Lamb. It is possible that you may be disappointed with him. It is—shall I say?—almost probable that you will be disappointed with him, at any rate partially. You will have expected more joy in him than you have received. I have referred in a previous chapter to the feeling of disappointment which often comes from first contacts with the classics. The neophyte is apt to find them—I may as well out with the word—dull. You may have found Lamb less diverting, less interesting, than you hoped. You may have had to whip yourself up again and again to the effort of reading him. In brief, Lamb has not, for you, justified his terrific reputation. If a classic is a classic because it gives *pleasure* to succeeding generations of the people who are most keenly interested in literature, and if Lamb frequently strikes you as dull, then evidently there is something wrong. The difficulty must be fairly fronted, and the fronting of it brings us to the very core of the business of actually forming the taste. If your taste were classical you would discover in Lamb a continual fascination; whereas what you in fact do discover in Lamb is a not unpleasant flatness, enlivened by a vague humour and an occasional pathos. You ought, according to theory, to be enthusiastic; but you are apathetic, or, at best, half-hearted. There is a gulf. How to cross it?

To cross it needs time and needs trouble. The following considerations may aid. In the first place, we have to remember that, in coming into the society of the classics in general and of Charles Lamb in particular, we are coming into the society of a mental superior. What happens usually in such a case? We can judge by recalling what happens when we are in the society of a mental inferior. We say things of which he misses the import; we joke, and he does not smile; what makes him laugh loudly seems to us horseplay or childish; he is blind to beauties which ravish us; he is ecstatic over what strikes us as crude; and his profound truths are for us trite commonplaces. His perceptions are relatively coarse; our perceptions are relatively subtle. We try to make him understand, to make him see, and if he is aware of his inferiority we may have some success. But if he is not aware of his inferiority, we soon hold our tongues and leave him alone in his self-satisfaction, convinced that there is nothing to be done with him. Every one of us has been through this experience with a mental inferior, for there is always a mental inferior handy, just as there is always a being more unhappy than we are. In approaching a classic, the true wisdom is to place ourselves in the position of the mental inferior, aware of mental inferiority, humbly stripping off all conceit, anxious to rise out of that inferiority. Recollect that we always regard as quite hopeless the mental inferior who does not suspect his own inferiority. Our attitude towards Lamb must be: "Charles Lamb was a greater man than I am, cleverer, sharper, subtler, finer, intellectually more powerful, and with keener eyes for beauty. I must brace myself to follow his lead." Our attitude must resemble that of one who cocks his ear and listens with all his soul for a distant sound.

To catch the sound we really must listen. That is to say, we must read carefully, with our faculties on the watch. We must read slowly and perseveringly. A classic has to be wooed and is worth the wooing. Further, we must disdain no assistance. I am not in favour of studying criticism of classics before the classics themselves. My notion is to study the work and the biography of a classical writer together, and then to read criticism afterwards. I think that in reprints of the classics the customary "critical introduction" ought to be put at the end, and not at the beginning, of the book. The classic should be allowed to make his own impression, how-ever faint, on the virginal mind of the reader. But after-wards let explanatory criticism be read as much as you please. Explanatory criticism is very useful; nearly as useful as pondering for oneself on what one has read! Explanatory criticism may throw one single gleam that lights up the entire subject.

My second consideration (in aid of crossing the gulf) touches the quality of the pleasure to be derived from a classic. It is never a violent pleasure. It is subtle, and it will wax in intensity, but the idea of violence is foreign to it. The artistic pleasures of an uncultivated mind are generally violent. They proceed from exaggeration in treatment, from a lack of balance, from attaching too great an importance to one aspect (usually superfi-cial), while quite ignoring another. They are gross, like the joy of Worcester sauce on the palate. Now, if there is one point common to all classics, it is the absence of exaggeration. The balanced sanity of a great mind makes impossible exaggeration, and, therefore, distor-tion. The beauty of a classic is not at all apt to knock you down. It will steal over you, rather. Many serious students are, I am convinced, discouraged in the early stages because they are expecting a wrong kind of plea-sure. They have abandoned Worcester sauce, and they miss it. They miss the coarse *tang*. They must realise that indulgence in the *tang* means the sure and total loss of sensitiveness—sensitiveness even to the *tang* it-self. They cannot have crudeness and fineness together. They must choose, remembering that while crudeness kills pleasure, fineness ever intensifies it.

8

SYSTEM IN HEADING

You have now definitely set sail on the sea of literature. You are afloat, and your anchor is up. I think I have given adequate warning of the dangers and disappointments which await the unwary and the sanguine. The enterprise in which you are engaged is not facile, nor is it short. I think I have sufficiently predicted that you will have your hours of woe, during which you may be inclined to send to perdition all writers, together with the inventor of printing. But if you have become really friendly with Lamb; if you know Lamb, or even half of him; if you have formed an image of him in your mind, and can, as it were, hear him brilliantly stuttering while you read his essays or letters, then certainly you are in a fit condition to proceed and you want to know in which direction you are to proceed. Yes, I have caught your terrified and protesting whisper: "I hope to heaven he isn't going to prescribe a Course of English Literature, because I feel I shall never be able to do it!" I am not. If your object in life was to be a University Extension Lecturer in English literature, then I should prescribe something drastic and desolating. But as your object, so far as I am concerned, is simply to obtain the highest and most tonic form of artistic pleasure of which you are capable, I shall not prescribe any regular course. Nay, I shall venture to dissuade you from any regular course. No man, and assuredly no beginner, can possibly pursue a historical course of literature without wasting a lot of weary time in acquiring mere knowledge which will yield neither pleasure nor advantage. In the choice of reading the individual must count; caprice must count, for caprice is often the truest index to the individuality. Stand defiantly on your own feet, and do not excuse yourself to yourself. You do not exist in order to honour literature by becoming an encyclopaedia of literature. Literature exists for your service. Wherever you happen to be, that, for you, is the centre of literature.

Still, for your own sake you must confine yourself for a long time to recognised classics, for reasons already explained. And though you should not follow a course, you must have a system or principle. Your native sagacity will tell you that caprice, left quite unfettered, will end by being quite ridiculous. The system which I recommend is embodied in this counsel: Let one thing lead to another. In the sea of literature every part communicates with every other part; there are no land-locked lakes. It was with an eye to this system that I originally recommended you to start with Lamb. Lamb, if you are his intimate, has already brought you into relations with a number of other prominent writers with whom you can in turn be intimate, and who will be particularly useful to you. Among these are Wordsworth, Coleridge, Southey, Hazlitt, and Leigh Hunt. You cannot know Lamb without knowing these men, and some of them are of the highest importance. From the circle of Lamb's own work you may go off at a tangent at various points, according to your inclination. If, for instance, you are drawn towards poetry, you cannot, in all English literature, make a better start than with Wordsworth. And Wordsworth will send you backwards to a comprehension of the poets against whose influence Wordsworth fought. When you have understood Wordsworth's and Coleridge's *Lyrical Ballads,* and Wordsworth's defence of them, you will be in a position to judge poetry in general. If, again, your mind hankers after an earlier and more romantic literature, Lamb's *Specimens of English Dramatic Poets Contemporary with Shakspere* has already, in an enchanting fashion, piloted you into a vast gulf of "the sea which is Shakspere."

Again, in Hazlitt and Leigh Hunt you will discover essayists inferior only to Lamb himself, and critics perhaps not inferior. Hazlitt is unsurpassed as a critic. His judgments are convincing and his enthusiasm of the most catching nature. Having arrived at Hazlitt or Leigh Hunt, you can branch off once more at any one of ten thousand points into still wider circles. And thus you may continue up and down the centuries as far as you like, yea, even to Chaucer. If you chance to read Hazlitt on *Chaucer and Spenser,* you will probably put your hat on instantly and go out and buy these authors; such is his communicating fire! I need not particularise further. Commencing with Lamb, and allowing one thing to lead to another, you cannot fail to be more and more impressed by the peculiar suitability to your needs of the Lamb entourage and the Lamb period. For Lamb lived in a time of universal rebirth in English literature. Wordsworth and Coleridge were re-creating poetry; Scott was re-creating the novel; Lamb was re-creating the human document; and Hazlitt, Coleridge, Leigh Hunt, and others were re-creating criticism. Sparks are flying all about the place, and it will be not less than a miracle if something combustible and indestructible in you does not take fire.

I have only one cautionary word to utter. You may be saying to yourself: "So long as I stick to classics I cannot go wrong." You can go wrong. You can, while reading naught but very fine stuff, commit the grave error of reading too much of one kind of stuff. Now there are two kinds, and only two kinds. These two kinds are not prose and poetry, nor are they divided the one from the other by any differences of form or of subject. They are the inspiring kind and the informing kind. *Lit* No other genuine division exists in literature. Emerson, I think, first clearly stated it. His terms were the literature of "power" and the literature of "knowledge." In nearly all great literature the two qualities are to be found in company, but one usually predominates over the other. An example of the exclusively inspiring kind is Coleridge's *Kubla Khan.* I cannot recall any first-class example of the purely informing kind. The nearest approach to it that I can name is Spencer's *First Principles,* which, however, is at least once highly inspiring. An example in which the inspiring quality predominates is *Ivanhoe;* and an example in which the informing quality predominates is Hazlitt's essays on Shakespeare's characters. You must avoid giving undue preference to the kind in which the inspiring quality predominates or to the kind in which the informing quality predominates. Too much of the one is enervating; too much of the other is desiccating. If you stick exclusively to the one you may become a mere debauchee of the emotions; if you stick exclusively to the other you may cease to live in any full sense. I do not say that you should hold the balance exactly even between the two kinds. Your taste will come into the scale. What I say is that neither kind must be neglected.

Lamb is an instance of a great writer whom anybody can understand and whom a majority of those who interest themselves in literature can more or less appreciate. He makes no excessive demand either on the intellect or on the faculty of sympathetic emotion. On both sides of Lamb, however, there lie literatures more difficult, more recondite. The "knowledge" side need not detain us here; it can be mastered by concentration and perseverance. But the "power" side, which comprises the supreme productions of genius, demands special consideration. You may have arrived at the point of keenly enjoying Lamb and yet be entirely unable to "see anything in" such writings as *Kubla Khan* or Milton's *Comus;* and as for *Hamlet* you may see nothing in it but a sanguinary tale "full of quotations." Nevertheless it is the supreme productions which are capable of yielding the supreme pleasures, and which *will* yield the supreme pleasures when the pass-key to them has been acquired. This pass-key is a comprehension of the nature of poetry.

9

VERSE

There is a word, a "name of fear," which rouses terror in the heart of the vast educated majority of the English-speaking race. The most valiant will fly at the mere utterance of that word. The most broad-minded will put their backs up against it. The most rash will not dare to affront it. I myself have seen it empty buildings that had been full; and I know that it will scatter a crowd more quickly than a hose-pipe, hornets, or the rumour of plague. Even to murmur it is to incur solitude, probably disdain, and possibly starvation, as historical examples show. That word is "poetry."

The profound objection of the average man to poetry can scarcely be exaggerated. And when I say the average man, I do not mean the "average sensual man"—any man who gets on to the top of the omnibus; I mean the average lettered man, the average man who does care a little for books and enjoys reading, and knows the classics by name and the popular writers by having read them. I am convinced that not one man in ten who reads, reads poetry—at any rate, knowingly. I am convinced, further, that not one man in ten who goes so far as knowingly to *buy* poetry ever reads it. You will find everywhere men who read very widely in prose, but who will say quite callously, "No, I never read poetry." If the sales of modern poetry, distinctly labelled as such, were to cease entirely to-morrow not a publisher would fail; scarcely a publisher would be affected; and not a poet would die—for I do not believe that a single modern English poet is living to-day on the current proceeds of his verse. For a country which possesses the greatest poetical literature in the world this condition of affairs is at least odd. What makes it odder is that, occasionally, very occasionally, the average lettered man will have a fit of idolatry for a fine poet, buying his books in tens of thousands, and bestowing upon him immense riches. As with Tennyson. And what makes it odder still is that, after all, the average lettered man does not truly dislike poetry; he only dislikes it when it takes a certain form. He will read poetry and enjoy it, provided he is not aware that it is poetry. Poetry can exist authentically either in prose or in verse. Give him poetry concealed in prose and there is a chance that, taken off his guard, he will appreciate it. But show him a page of verse, and he will be ready to send for a policeman. The reason of this is that, though poetry may come to pass either in prose or in verse, it does actually happen far more frequently in verse than in prose; nearly all the very greatest poetry is in verse; verse is identified with the very greatest poetry, and the very greatest poetry can only be understood and savoured by people who have put themselves through a considerable mental discipline. To others it is an exasperating weariness. Hence chiefly the fearful prejudice of the average lettered man against the mere form of verse.

The formation of literary taste cannot be completed until that prejudice has been conquered. My very difficult task is to suggest a method of conquering it. I address myself exclusively to the large class of people who, if they are honest, will declare that, while they enjoy novels, essays, and history, they cannot "stand" verse. The case is extremely delicate, like all nervous cases. It is useless to employ the arts of reasoning, for the matter has got beyond logic; it is instinctive. Perfectly futile to assure you that verse will yield a higher percentage of pleasure than prose! You will reply: "We believe you, but that doesn't help us." Therefore I shall not argue. I shall venture to prescribe a curative treatment (doctors do not argue); and I beg you to follow it exactly, keeping your nerve and your calm. Loss of self-control might lead to panic, and panic would be fatal.

First: Forget as completely as you can all your present notions about the nature of verse and poetry. Take a sponge and wipe the slate of your mind. In particular, do not harass yourself by thoughts of metre and verse forms. Second: Read William Hazlitt's essay "On Poetry in General." This essay is the first in the book entitled *Lectures on the English Poets*. It can be bought in various forms. I think the cheapest satisfactory edition is in Routledge's "New Universal Library" (price 1s. net). I might have composed an essay of my own on the real harmless nature of poetry in general, but it could only have been an echo and a deterioration of Hazlitt's. He has put the truth about poetry in a way as interesting, clear, and reassuring as anyone is ever likely to put it. I do not expect, however, that you will instantly gather the full message and enthusiasm of the essay. It will probably seem to you not to "hang together." Still, it will leave bright bits of ideas in your mind. Third: After a week's interval read the essay again. On a second perusal it will appear more persuasive to you.

Fourth: Open the Bible and read the fortieth chapter of Isaiah. It is the chapter which begins, "Comfort ye, comfort ye, my people," and ends, "They shall run and not be weary, and they shall walk and not faint." This chapter will doubtless be more or less familiar to you. It cannot fail (whatever your particular *ism*) to impress you, to generate in your mind sensations which you recognise to be of a lofty and unusual order, and which you will admit to be pleasurable. You will probably agree that the result of reading this chapter (even if your particular *ism* is opposed to its authority) is finer than the result of reading a short story in a magazine or even an essay by Charles Lamb. Now the pleasurable sensations induced by the fortieth chapter of Isaiah are among the sensations usually induced by high-class poetry. The writer of it was a very great poet, and what he wrote is a very great poem. Fifth: After having read it, go back to Hazlitt, and see if you can find anything in Hazlitt's lecture which throws light on the psychology of your own emotions upon reading Isaiah.

Sixth: The next step is into unmistakable verse. It is to read one of Wordsworth's short narrative poems, *The Brothers*. There are editions of Wordsworth at a shilling, but I should advise the "Golden Treasury" Wordsworth (2s. 6d. net), because it contains the famous essay by Matthew Arnold, who made the selection. I want you to read this poem aloud. You will probably have to hide yourself somewhere in order to do so, for, of course, you would not, as yet, care to be overheard spouting poetry. Be good enough to forget that *The Brothers* is poetry. *The Brothers* is a short story, with a plain, clear plot. Read it as such. Read it simply for the story. It is very important at this critical stage that you should not embarrass your mind with preoccupations as to the *form* in which Wordsworth has told his story. Wordsworth's object was to tell a story as well as he could: just that. In reading aloud do not pay any more attention to the metre than you feel naturally inclined to pay. After a few lines the metre will present itself to you. Do not worry as to what kind of metre it is. When you have finished the perusal, examine your sensations....

Your sensations after reading this poem, and perhaps one or two other narrative poems of Wordsworth, such as *Michael,* will be different from the sensations produced in you by reading an ordinary, or even a very extraordinary, short story in prose. They may not be so sharp, so clear and piquant, but they will probably be, in their mysteriousness and their vagueness, more impressive. I do not say that they will be diverting. I do not go so far as to say that they will strike you as pleasing sensations. (Be it remembered that I am addressing myself to an imaginary tyro in poetry.) I would qualify them as being "disturbing." Well, to disturb the spirit is one of the greatest aims of art. And a disturbance of spirit is one of the finest pleasures that a highly-organised man can enjoy. But this truth can only be really learnt by the repetitions of experience. As an aid to the more exhaustive examination of your feelings under Wordsworth, in order that you may better understand what he was trying to effect in you, and the means which he employed, I must direct you to Wordsworth himself. Wordsworth, in addition to being a poet, was unsurpassed as a critic of poetry. What Hazlitt does for poetry in the way of creating enthusiasm Wordsworth does in the way of philosophic explanation. And Wordsworth's explanations of the theory and practice of poetry are written for the plain man. They pass the comprehension of nobody, and their direct, unassuming, and calm simplicity is extremely persuasive. Wordsworth's chief essays in throwing light on himself are the "Advertisement," "Preface," and "Appendix" to *Lyrical Ballads;* the letters to Lady Beaumont and "the Friend" and the "Preface" to the Poems dated 1815. All this matter is strangely interesting and of immense educational value. It is the first-class expert talking at ease about his subject. The essays relating to *Lyrical Ballads* will be the most useful for you. You will discover these precious documents in a volume entitled *Wordsworth's Literary Criticism* (published by Henry Frowde, 2s. 6d.), edited by that distinguished Wordsworthian Mr. Nowell C. Smith. It is essential that the student of poetry should become possessed, honestly or dishonestly, either of this volume or of the matter which it contains. There is, by the way, a volume of Wordsworth's prose in the Scott Library (1s.). Those who have not read Wordsworth on poetry can have no idea of the naive charm and the helpful radiance of his expounding. I feel that I cannot too strongly press Wordsworth's criticism upon you.

Between Wordsworth and Hazlitt you will learn all that it behoves you to know of the nature, the aims, and the results of poetry. It is no part of my scheme to dot the "i's" and cross the "t's" of Wordsworth and Hazlitt. I best fulfil my purpose in urgently referring you to them. I have only a single point of my own to make—a psychological detail. One of the main obstacles to the cultivation of poetry in the average sensible man is an absurdly inflated notion of the ridiculous. At the bottom of that man's mind is the idea that poetry is "silly." He also finds it exaggerated and artificial; but these two accusations against poetry can be satisfactorily answered. The charge of silliness, of being ridiculous, however, cannot be refuted by argument. There is no logical answer to a guffaw. This sense of the ridiculous is merely a bad, infantile habit, in itself grotesquely ridiculous. You may see it particularly in the theatre. Not the greatest dramatist, not the greatest composer, not the greatest actor can prevent an audience from laughing uproariously at a tragic moment if a cat walks across the stage. But why ruin the scene by laughter? Simply because the majority of any audience is artistically childish. This sense of the ridiculous can only be crushed by the exercise of moral force. It can only be cowed. If you are inclined to laugh when a poet expresses himself more powerfully than you express yourself, when a poet talks about feelings which are not usually mentioned in daily papers, when a poet uses words and images which lie outside your vocabulary and range of thought, then you had better take yourself in hand. You have to decide whether you will be on the side of the angels or on the side of the nincompoops. There is no surer sign of imperfect development than the impulse to snigger at what is unusual, naive, or exuberant. And if you choose to do so, you can detect the cat walking across the stage in the sublimest passages of literature. But more advanced souls will grieve for you.

The study of Wordsworth's criticism makes the seventh step in my course of treatment. The eighth is to return to those poems of Wordsworth's which you have already perused, and read them again in the full light of the author's defence and explanation. Read as much Wordsworth as you find you can assimilate, but do not attempt either of his long poems. The time, however, is now come for a long poem. I began by advising narrative poetry for the neophyte, and I shall persevere with the prescription. I mean narrative poetry in the restricted sense; for epic poetry is narrative. *Paradise Lost* is narrative; so is *The Prelude*. I suggest neither of these great works. My choice falls on Elizabeth Browning's *Aurora Leigh*. If you once work yourself "into" this poem, interesting yourself primarily (as with Wordsworth) in the events of the story, and not allowing yourself to be obsessed by the fact that what you are reading is "poetry"—if you do this, you are not likely to leave it unfinished. And before you reach the end you will have encountered *en route* pretty nearly all the moods of poetry that exist: tragic, humorous, ironic, elegiac, lyric—everything. You will have a comprehensive acquaintance with a poet's mind. I guarantee that you will come safely through if you treat the work as a novel. For a novel it effectively is, and a better one than any written by Charlotte Bronte or George Eliot. In reading, it would be well to mark, or take note of, the passages which give you the most pleasure, and then to compare these passages with the passages selected for praise by some authoritative critic. *Aurora Leigh* can be got in the "Temple Classics" (1s. 6d.), or in the "Canterbury Poets" (1s.). The indispensable biographical information about Mrs. Browning can be obtained from Mr. J.H. Ingram's short Life of her in the "Eminent Women" Series (1s. 6d.), or from *Robert Browning*, by William Sharp ("Great Writers" Series, 1s.).

This accomplished, you may begin to choose your poets. Going back to Hazlitt, you will see that he deals with, among others, Chaucer, Spenser, Shakespeare, Milton, Dryden, Pope, Chatterton, Burns, and the Lake School. You might select one of these, and read under his guidance. Said Wordsworth: "I was impressed by the conviction that there were four English poets whom I must have continually before me as examples—Chaucer, Shakespeare, Spenser, and Milton." (A word to the wise!) Wordsworth makes a fifth to these four. Concurrently with the careful, enthusiastic study of one of the undisputed classics, modern verse should be read. (I beg you to accept the following statement: that if the study of classical poetry inspires you with a distaste for modern poetry, then there is something seriously wrong in the method of your development.) You may at this stage (and not before) commence an inquiry into questions of rhythm, verse-structure, and rhyme. There is, I believe, no good, concise, cheap handbook to English prosody; yet such a manual is greatly needed. The only one with which I am acquainted is Tom Hood the younger's *Rules of Rhyme: A Guide to English Versification*. Again, the introduction to Walker's *Rhyming Dictionary* gives a fairly clear elementary account of the subject. Ruskin also has written an excellent essay on verse-rhythms. With a manual in front of you, you can acquire in a couple of hours a knowledge of the formal principles in which the music of English verse is rooted. The business is trifling. But the business of appreciating the inmost spirit of the greatest verse is tremendous and lifelong. It is not something that can be "got up."

10

BROAD COUNSELS

I have now set down what appear to me to be the necessary considerations, recommendations, exhortations, and dehortations in aid of this delicate and arduous enterprise of forming the literary taste. I have dealt with the theory of literature, with the psychology of the author, and—quite as important—with the psychology of the reader. I have tried to explain the author to the reader and the reader to himself. To go into further detail would be to exceed my original intention, with no hope of ever bringing the constantly-enlarging scheme to a logical conclusion. My aim is not to provide a map, but a compass—two very different instruments. In the way of general advice it remains for me only to put before you three counsels which apply more broadly than any I have yet offered to the business of reading.

You have within yourself a touchstone by which finally you can, and you must, test every book that your brain is capable of comprehending. Does the book seem to you to be sincere and true? If it does, then you need not worry about your immediate feelings, or the possible future consequences of the book. You will ultimately like the book, and you will be justified in liking it. Honesty, in literature as in life, is the quality that counts first and counts last. But beware of your immediate feelings. Truth is not always pleasant. The first glimpse of truth is, indeed, usually so disconcerting as to be positively unpleasant, and our impulse is to tell it to go away, for we will have no truck with it. If a book arouses your genuine contempt, you may dismiss it from your mind. Take heed, however, lest you confuse contempt with anger. If a book really moves you to anger, the chances are that it is a good book. Most good books have begun by causing anger which disguised itself as contempt. Demanding honesty from your authors, you must see that you render it yourself. And to be honest with oneself is not so simple as it appears. One's sensations and one's sentiments must be examined with detachment. When you have violently flung down a book, listen whether you can hear a faint voice saying within you: "It's true, though!" And if you catch the whisper, better yield to it as quickly as you can. For sooner or later the voice will win. Similarly, when you are hugging a book, keep your ear cocked for the secret warning: "Yes, but it isn't true." For bad books, by flattering you, by caressing, by appealing to the weak or the base in you, will often persuade you what fine and splendid books they are. (Of course, I use the word "true" in a wide and essential significance. I do not necessarily mean true to literal fact; I mean true to the plane of experience in which the book moves. The truthfulness of *Ivanhoe,* for example, cannot be estimated by the same standards as the truthfulness of Stubbs's *Constitutional History.*) In reading a book, a sincere questioning of oneself, "Is it true?" and a loyal abiding by the answer, will help more surely than any other process of ratiocination to form the taste. I will not assert that this question and answer are all-sufficient. A true book is not always great. But a great book is never untrue.

My second counsel is: In your reading you must have in view some definite aim—some aim other than the wish to derive pleasure. I conceive that to give pleasure is the highest end of any work of art, because the pleasure procured from any art is tonic, and transforms the life into which it enters. But the maximum of pleasure can only be obtained by regular effort, and regular effort implies the organisation of that effort. Open-air walking is a glorious exercise; it is the walking itself which is glorious. Nevertheless, when setting out for walking exercise, the sane man generally has a subsidiary aim in view. He says to himself either that he will reach a given point, or that he will progress at a given speed for a given distance, or that he will remain on his feet for a given time. He organises his effort, partly in order that he may combine some other advantage with the advantage of walking, but principally in order to be sure that the effort shall be an adequate effort. The same with reading. Your paramount aim in poring over literature is to enjoy, but you will not fully achieve that aim unless you have also a subsidiary aim which necessitates the measurement of your energy. Your subsidiary aim may be aesthetic, moral, political, religious, scientific, erudite; you may devote yourself to a man, a topic, an epoch, a nation, a branch of literature, an idea—you have the widest latitude in the choice of an objective; but a definite objective you must have. In my earlier remarks as to method in reading, I advocated, without insisting on, regular hours for study. But I both advocate and insist on the fixing of a date for the accomplishment of an allotted task. As an instance, it is not enough to say: "I will inform myself completely as to the Lake School." It is necessary to say: "I will inform myself completely as to the Lake School before I am a year older." Without this precautionary steeling of the resolution the risk of a humiliating collapse into futility is enormously magnified.

My third counsel is: Buy a library. It is obvious that you cannot read unless you have books. I began by urging the constant purchase of books—any books of approved quality, without reference to their immediate bearing upon your particular case. The moment has now come to inform you plainly that a bookman is, amongst other things, a man who possesses many books. A man who does not possess many books is not a bookman. For years literary authorities have been favouring the literary public with wondrously selected lists of "the best books"—the best novels, the best histories, the best poems, the best works of philosophy—or the hundred best or the fifty best of all sorts. The fatal disadvantage of such lists is that they leave out large quantities of literature which is admittedly first-class. The bookman cannot content himself with a selected library. He wants, as a minimum, a library reasonably complete in all departments. With such a basis acquired, he can afterwards wander into those special byways of book-buying which happen to suit his special predilections. Every Englishman who is interested in any branch of his native literature, and who respects himself, ought to own a comprehensive and inclusive library of English literature, in comely and adequate editions. You may suppose that this counsel is a counsel of perfection. It is not. Mark Pattison laid down a rule that he who desired the name of book-lover must spend five per cent. of his income on books. The proposal does not seem extravagant, but even on a smaller percentage than five the average reader of these pages may become the owner, in a comparatively short space of time, of a reasonably complete English library, by which I mean a library containing the complete works of the supreme geniuses, representative important works of all the first-class men in all departments, and specimen works of all the men of the second rank whose reputation is really a living reputation to-day. The scheme for a library, which I now present, begins before Chaucer and ends with George Gissing, and I am fairly sure that the majority of people will be startled at the total inexpensiveness of it. So far as I am aware, no such scheme has ever been printed before.

11

AN ENGLISH LIBRARY: PERIOD I

(For much counsel and correction in the matter of editions and prices I am indebted to my old and valued friend, Charles Young, head of the firm of Lamley & Co., booksellers, South Kensington.)

For the purposes of book-buying, I divide English literature, not strictly into historical epochs, but into three periods which, while scarcely arbitrary from the historical point of view, have nevertheless been calculated according to the space which they will occupy on the shelves and to the demands which they will make on the purse:

I. From the beginning to John Dryden, or roughly, to the end of the seventeenth century. *start 1699*

II. From William Congreve to Jane Austen, or roughly, the eighteenth century. *1700 → 1799*

III. Sir Walter Scott to the last deceased author who is recognised as a classic, or roughly, the nineteenth century. *1800 → 1899*

Period III. will bulk the largest and cost the most; not necessarily because it contains more absolutely great books than the other periods (though in my opinion it *does*), but because it is nearest to us, and therefore fullest of interest for us.

I have not confined my choice to books of purely literary interest—that is to say, to works which are primarily works of literary art. Literature is the vehicle of philosophy, science, morals, religion, and history; and a library which aspires to be complete must comprise, in addition to imaginative works, all these branches of intellectual activity. Comprising all these branches, it cannot avoid comprising works of which the purely literary interest is almost nil.

On the other hand, I have excluded from consideration:—

I. Works whose sole importance is that they form a link in the chain of development. For example, nearly all the productions of authors between Chaucer and the beginning of the Elizabethan period, such as Gower, Hoccleve, and Skelton, whose works, for sufficient reason, are read only by professors and students who mean to be professors.

II. Works not originally written in English, such as the works of that very great philosopher Roger Bacon, of whom this isle ought to be prouder than it is. To this rule, however, I have been constrained to make a few exceptions. Sir Thomas More's *Utopia* was written in Latin, but one does not easily conceive a library to be complete without it. And could one exclude Sir Isaac Newton's *Principia,* the masterpiece of the greatest physicist that the world has ever seen? The law of gravity ought to have, and does have, a powerful sentimental interest for us.

III. Translations from foreign literature into English.

Here, then, are the lists for the first period:

PROSE WRITERS	L	s.	d.
Bede, *Ecclesiastical History:* Temple Classics.	0	1	6
Sir Thomas Malory, *Morte d'Arthur:* Everyman's Library (4 vols.)	0	4	0
Sir Thomas More, *Utopia:* Scott Library	0	1	0
George Cavendish, *Life of Cardinal Wolsey:* New Universal Library.	0	1	0
Richard Hakluyt, *Voyages:* Everyman's Library (8 vols.)	0	8	0
Richard Hooker, *Ecclesiastical Polity:* Everyman's Library (2 vols.)	0	2	0
Francis Bacon, *Works:* Newnes's Thinpaper Classics.	0	2	0
Thomas Dekker, *Gull's Horn-Book:* King's Classics.	0	1	6
Lord Herbert of Cherbury, *Autobiography:* Scott Library.	0	1	0
John Selden, *Table-Talk:* New Universal Library.	0	1	0
Thomas Hobbes, *Leviathan:* New Universal Library.	0	1	0
James Howell, *Familiar Letters:* Temple Classics (3 vols.)	0	4	6
Sir Thomas Browne, *Religio Medici,* etc.: Everyman's Library.	0	1	0
Jeremy Taylor, *Holy Living and Holy Dying:* Temple Classics (3 vols.)	0	4	6
Izaak Walton, *Compleat Angler:* Everyman's Library.	0	1	0
John Bunyan, *Pilgrim's Progress:* World's Classics.	0	1	0

	L	s.	d.
Sir William Temple, *Essay on Gardens of Epicurus:* King's Classics.	o	1	6
John Evelyn, *Diary:* Everyman's Library (2 vols.)	o	2	o
Samuel Pepys, *Diary:* Everyman's Library (2 vols.)	o	2	o
	L 2	1	6

The principal omission from the above list is *The Paston Letters,* which I should probably have included had the enterprise of publishers been sufficient to put an edition on the market at a cheap price. Other omissions include the works of Caxton and Wyclif, and such books as Camden's *Britannia,* Ascham's *Schoolmaster,* and Fuller's *Worthies,* whose lack of first-rate value as literature is not adequately compensated by their historical interest. As to the Bible, in the first place it is a translation, and in the second I assume that you already possess a copy.

POETS	L	s.	d.
Beowulf, Routledge's London Library	o	2	6
GEOFFREY CHAUCER, *Works:* Globe Edition	o	3	6
Nicolas Udall, *Ralph Roister-Doister:* Temple Dramatists	o	1	o
EDMUND SPENSER, *Works:* Globe Edition	o	3	6
Thomas Lodge, *Rosalynde:* Caxton Series	o	1	o
Robert Greene, *Tragical Reign of Selimus:* Temple Dramatists	o	1	o
Michael Drayton, *Poems:* Newnes's Pocket Classics	o	8	6
CHRISTOPHER MARLOWE, *Works:* New Universal Library	o	1	o
WILLIAM SHAKESPEARE, *Works:* Globe Edition	o	3	6

Thomas Campion, *Poems:* Muses' Library	o	1	o
Ben Jonson, *Plays:* Canterbury Poets	o	1	o
John Donne, *Poems:* Muses' Library (2 vols.)	o	2	o
John Webster, Cyril Tourneur, *Plays:* Mermaid Series	o	2	6
Philip Massinger, *Plays:* Cunningham Edition	o	3	6
Beaumont and Fletcher, *Plays:* a Selection Canterbury Poets	o	1	o
John Ford, *Plays:* Mermaid Series	o	2	6
George Herbert, *The Temple:* Everyman's Library	o	1	o
ROBERT HERRICK, *Poems:* Muses' Library (2 vols.)	o	2	o
Edmund Waller, *Poems:* Muses' Library (2 vols.)	o	2	o
Sir John Suckling, *Poems:* Muses' Library	o	1	o
Abraham Cowley, *English Poems:* Cambridge University Press	o	4	6
Richard Crashaw, *Poems:* Muses' Library	o	1	o
Henry Vaughan, *Poems:* Methuen's Little Library	o	1	6
Samuel Butler, *Hudibras:* Cambridge University Press	o	4	6
JOHN MILTON, *Poetical Works:* Oxford Cheap Edition	o	2	o
JOHN MILTON, *Select Prose Works:* Scott Library	o	1	o
Andrew Marvell, *Poems:* Methuen's Little Library	o	1	6
John Dryden, *Poetical Works:* Globe Edition	o	3	6

[Thomas Percy], *Reliques of Ancient English Poetry:* Everyman's Library (2 vols.)	0	2	0
Arber's *"Spenser" Anthology:* Oxford University Press	0	2	0
Arber's *"Jonson" Anthology:* Oxford University Press	0	2	0
Arber's *"Shakspere" Anthology:* Oxford University Press	0	2	0
	L 3	7	6

There were a number of brilliant minor writers in the seventeenth century whose best work, often trifling in bulk, either scarcely merits the acquisition of a separate volume for each author, or cannot be obtained at all in a modern edition. Such authors, however, may not be utterly neglected in the formation of a library. It is to meet this difficulty that I have included the last three volumes on the above list. Professor Arber's anthologies are full of rare pieces, and comprise admirable specimens of the verse of Samuel Daniel, Giles Fletcher, Countess of Pembroke, James I., George Peele, Sir Walter Raleigh, Thomas Sackville, Sir Philip Sidney, Drummond of Hawthornden, Thomas Heywood, George Wither, Sir Henry Wotton, Sir William Davenant, Thomas Randolph, Frances Quarles, James Shirley, and other greater and lesser poets.

I have included all the important Elizabethan dramatists except John Marston, all the editions of whose works, according to my researches, are out of print.

In the Elizabethan and Jacobean periods talent was so extraordinarily plentiful that the standard of excellence is quite properly raised, and certain authors are thus relegated to the third, or excluded, class who in a less fertile period would have counted as at least second-class.

SUMMARY OF THE FIRST PERIOD.			L	s.	d.
19 prose authors in	36	volumes costing	2	1	6
29 poets in	36	" "		3	7	6
48	72		L 5	9	0

In addition, scores of authors of genuine interest are represented in the anthologies.

The prices given are gross, and in many instances there is a 25 per cent. discount to come off. All the volumes can be procured immediately at any bookseller's.

12

AN ENGLISH LIBRARY: PERIOD II

After dealing with the formation of a library of authors up to John Dryden, I must logically arrange next a scheme for the period covered roughly by the eighteenth century. There is, however, no reason why the student in quest of a library should follow the chronological order. Indeed, I should advise him to attack the nineteenth century before the eighteenth, for the reason that, unless his taste happens to be peculiarly "Augustan," he will obtain a more immediate satisfaction and profit from his acquisitions in the nineteenth century than in the eighteenth. There is in eighteenth-century literature a considerable proportion of what I may term "unattractive excellence," which one must have for the purposes of completeness, but which may await actual perusal until more pressing and more human books have been read. I have particularly in mind the philosophical authors of the century.

PROSE WRITERS.	L	s.	d.
JOHN LOCKE, *Philosophical Works:* Bohn's Edition (2 vols.)	0	7	0
SIR ISAAC NEWTON, *Principia* (sections 1, 2, and 3): Macmillans	0	12	0

Gilbert Burnet, *History of His Own Time:* Everyman's Library	o 1 o
William Wycherley, *Best Plays:* Mermaid Series	o 2 6
WILLIAM CONGREVE, *Best Plays:* Mermaid Series	o 2 6
Jonathan Swift, *Tale of a Tub:* Scott Library	o 1 o
Jonathan Swift, *Gulliver's Travels:* Temple Classics	o 1 6
DANIEL DEFOE, *Robinson Crusoe:* World's Classics	o 1 o
DANIEL DEFOE, *Journal of the Plague Year:* Everyman's Library	o 1 o
Joseph Addison, Sir Richard Steele, *Essays:* Scott Library	o 1 o
William Law, *Serious Call:* Everyman's Library	o 1 o
Lady Mary W. Montagu, *Letters:* Everyman's Library	o 1 o
George Berkeley, *Principles of Human Knowledge:* New Universal Library	o 1 o
SAMUEL RICHARDSON, *Clarissa* (abridged): Routledge's Edition	o 2 o
John Wesley, *Journal:* Everyman's Library (4 vols.)	o 4 o
HENRY FIELDING, *Tom Jones:* Routledge's Edition	o 2 o
HENRY FIELDING, *Amelia:* Routledge's Edition	o 2 o
HENRY FIELDING, *Joseph Andrews:* Routledge's Edition	o 2 o
David Hume, *Essays:* World's Classics	o 1 o

LAURENCE STERNE, *Tristram Shandy:* World's Classics	0	1	0
LAURENCE STERNE, *Sentimental Journey:* New Universal Library	0	1	0
Horace Walpole, *Castle of Otranto:* King's Classics	0	1	6
Tobias Smollett, *Humphrey Clinker:* Routledge's Edition	0	2	0
Tobias Smollett, *Travels through France and Italy:* World's Classics	0	1	0
ADAM SMITH, *Wealth of Nations:* World's Classics (2 vols.)	0	2	0
Samuel Johnson, *Lives of the Poets:* World's Classics (2 vols.)	0	2	0
Samuel Johnson, *Rasselas:* New Universal Library	0	1	0
JAMES BOSWELL, *Life of Johnson:* Everyman's Library (2 vols.)	0	2	0
Oliver Goldsmith, *Works:* Globe Edition	0	3	6
Henry Mackenzie, *The Man of Feeling:* Cassell's National Library	0	0	6
Sir Joshua Reynolds, *Discourses on Art:* Scott Library	0	1	0
Edmund Burke, *Reflections on the French Revolution:* Scott Library	0	1	0
Edmund Burke, *Thoughts on the Present Discontents:* New Universal Library	0	1	0
EDWARD GIBBON, *Decline and Fall of the Roman Empire:* World's Classics (7 vols.)	0	7	0
Thomas Paine, *Rights of Man:* Watts and Co.'s Edition	0	1	0
RICHARD BRINSLEY SHERIDAN, *Plays:* World's Classics	0	1	0

	L	s.	d.
Fanny Burney, *Evelina:* Everyman's Library	0	1	0
Gilbert White, *Natural History of Selborne:* Everyman's Library	0	1	0
Arthur Young, *Travels in France:* York Library	0	2	0
Mungo Park, *Travels:* Everyman's Library	0	1	0
Jeremy Bentham, *Introduction to the Principles of Morals:* Clarendon Press	0	6	6
THOMAS ROBERT MALTHUS, *Essay on the Principle of Population:* Ward, Lock's Edition	0	3	0
William Godwin, *Caleb Williams:* Newnes's Edition	0	1	0
Maria Edgeworth, *Helen:* Macmillan's Illustrated Edition	0	2	6
JANE AUSTEN, *Novels:* Nelson's New Century Library (2 vols.)	0	4	0
James Morier, *Hadji Baba:* Macmillan's Illustrated Novels	0	2	6
	L 5	1	0

The principal omissions here are Jeremy Collier, whose outcry against the immorality of the stage is his slender title to remembrance; Richard Bentley, whose scholarship principally died with him, and whose chief works are no longer current; and "Junius," who would have been deservedly forgotten long ago had there been a contemporaneous Sherlock Holmes to ferret out his identity.

POETS.	L	s.	d.
Thomas Otway, *Venice Preserved:* Temple Dramatists	0	1	0
Matthew Prior, *Poems on Several Occasions:* Cambridge English Classics	0	4	6

John Gay, *Poems:* Muses' Library (2 vols.)	0	2	0
ALEXANDER POPE, *Works:* Globe Edition	0	3	0
Isaac Watts, *Hymns:* Any hymn-book	0	1	0
James Thomson, *The Seasons:* Muses' Library	0	1	0
Charles Wesley, *Hymns:* Any hymn-book	0	1	0
THOMAS GRAY, Samuel Johnson, William Collins, *Poems:* Muses' Library	0	1	0
James Macpherson (Ossian), *Poems:* Canterbury Poets	0	1	0
THOMAS CHATTERTON, *Poems:* Muses' Library (2 vols.)	0	2	0
WILLIAM COWPER, *Poems:* Canterbury Poets	0	1	0
WILLIAM COWPER, *Letters:* World's Classics	0	1	0
George Crabbe, *Poems:* Methuen's Little Library	0	1	6
WILLIAM BLAKE, *Poems:* Muses' Library	0	1	0
William Lisle Bowles, Hartley Coleridge, *Poems:* Canterbury Poets	0	1	0
ROBERT BURNS, *Works:* Globe Edition	0	3	6
	L 1	7	0

SUMMARY OF THE PERIOD.

39	prose writers in	60 volumes, costing	L	5	1	0
18	poets "	18 " "		1	7	0
57		78	L	6	8	0

13

AN ENGLISH LIBRARY: PERIOD III

The catalogue of necessary authors of this third and last period being so long, it is convenient to divide the prose writers into Imaginative and Non-imaginative.

In the latter half of the period the question of copyright affects our scheme to a certain extent, because it affects prices. Fortunately it is the fact that no single book of recognised first-rate general importance is conspicuously dear. Nevertheless, I have encountered difficulties in the second rank; I have dealt with them in a spirit of compromise. I think I may say that, though I should have included a few more authors had their books been obtainable at a reasonable price, I have omitted none that I consider indispensable to a thoroughly representative collection. No living author is included.

Where I do not specify the edition of a book the original copyright edition is meant.

PROSE WRITERS: IMAGINATIVE.	L	s.	d.
SIR WALTER SCOTT, *Waverley, Heart of Midlothian, Quentin Durward, Red-gauntlet, Ivanhoe:* Everyman's Library (5 vols.)	0	5	0

SIR WALTER SCOTT, *Marmion,* etc.: Canterbury Poets	0	1	0
Charles Lamb, *Works in Prose and Verse:* Clarendon Press (2 vols.)	0	4	0
Charles Lamb, *Letters:* Newnes's Thin Paper Classics	0	2	0
Walter Savage Landor, *Imaginary Conversations:* Scott Library	0	1	0
Walter Savage Landor, *Poems:* Canterbury Poets	0	1	0
Leigh Hunt, *Essays and Sketches:* World's Classics	0	1	0
Thomas Love Peacock, *Principal Novels:* New Universal Library (2 vols.)	0	2	0
Mary Russell Mitford, *Our Village:* Scott Library	0	1	0
Michael Scott, *Tom Cringle's Log:* Macmillan's Illustrated Novels	0	2	6
Frederick Marryat, *Mr. Midshipman Easy:* Everyman's Library	0	1	0
John Galt, *Annals of the Parish:* Everyman's Library	0	1	0
Susan Ferrier, *Marriage:* Routledge's edition	0	2	0
Douglas Jerrold, *Mrs. Caudle's Curtain Lectures:* World's Classics	0	1	0
Lord Lytton, *Last Days of Pompeii:* Everyman's Library	0	1	0
William Carleton, *Stories:* Scott Library	0	1	0
Charles James Lever, *Harry Lorrequer*: Everyman's Library	0	1	0
Harrison Ainsworth, *The Tower of London:* New Universal Library	0	1	0
George Henry Borrow, *Bible in Spain, Lavengro:* New Universal Library (2 vols.)	0	2	0

Lord Beaconsfield, *Sybil, Coningsby:* Lane's New Pocket Library (2 vols.)	0	2	0
W.M. THACKERAY, *Vanity Fair, Esmond:* Everyman's Library (2 vols.)	0	2	0
W.M. THACKERAY, *Barry Lyndon,* and *Roundabout Papers,* etc.: Nelson's New Century Library	0	2	0
CHARLES DICKENS, *Works:* Everyman's Library (18 vols.)	0	18	0
Charles Reade, *The Cloister and the Hearth:* Everyman's Library	0	1	0
Anthony Trollope, *Barchester Towers, Framley Parsonage:* Lane's New Pocket Library (2 vols.)	0	2	0
Charles Kingsley, *Westward Ho!:* Everyman's Library	0	1	0
Henry Kingsley, *Ravenshoe:* Everyman's Library	0	1	0
Charlotte Bronte, *Jane Eyre, Shirley, Villette, Professor, and Poems:* World's Classics (4 vols.)	0	4	0
Emily Bronte, *Wuthering Heights:* World's Classics	0	1	0
Elizabeth Gaskell, *Cranford:* World's Classics	0	1	0
Elizabeth Gaskell, *Life of Charlotte Bronte*	0	2	6
George Eliot, *Adam Bede, Silas Marner, The Mill on the Floss:* Everyman's Library (3 vols.)	0	3	0
G.J. Whyte-Melville, *The Gladiators:* New Universal Library	0	1	0
Alexander Smith, *Dreamthorpe:* New Universal Library	0	1	0
George Macdonald, *Malcolm*	0	1	6

Walter Pater, *Imaginary Portraits*	o	6	o
Wilkie Collins, *The Woman in White*	o	1	o
R.D. Blackmore, *Lorna Doone:* Everyman's Library	o	1	o
Samuel Butler, *Erewhon:* Fifield's Edition	o	2	6
Laurence Oliphant, *Altiora Peto*	o	3	6
Margaret Oliphant, *Salem Chapel:* Everyman's Library	o	1	o
Richard Jefferies, *Story of My Heart*	o	2	o
Lewis Carroll, *Alice in Wonderland:* Macmillan's Cheap Edition	o	1	o
John Henry Shorthouse, *John Inglesant:* Macmillan's Pocket Classics	o	2	o
R.L. Stevenson, *Master of Ballantrae, Virginibus Puerisque:* Pocket Edition (2 vols.)	o	4	o
George Gissing, *The Odd Women:* Popular Edition (bound)	o	o	7
	L 5	o	1

Names such as those of Charlotte Yonge and Dinah Craik are omitted intentionally.

PROSE WRITERS: NON-IMAGINATIVE.	L	s.	d.
William Hazlitt, *Spirit of the Age:* World's Classics	o	1	o
William Hazlitt, *English Poets and Comic Writers:* Bohn's Library	o	3	6
Francis Jeffrey, *Essays from Edinburgh Review:* New Universal Library	o	1	o
Thomas de Quincey, *Confessions of an English Opium-eater,* etc.: Scott Library	o	1	o
Sydney Smith, *Selected Papers:* Scott Library	o	1	o

George Finlay, *Byzantine Empire:* Everyman's Library	o	1	o
John G. Lockhart, *Life of Scott:* Everyman's Library	o	1	o
Agnes Strickland, *Life of Queen Elizabeth:* Everyman's Library	o	1	o
Hugh Miller, *Old Red Sandstone:* Everyman's Library	o	1	o
J.H. Newman, *Apologia pro vita sua:* New Universal Library	o	1	o
Lord Macaulay, *History of England,* (3), *Essays* (2): Everyman's Library (5 vols.)	o	5	o
A.P. Stanley, *Memorials of Canterbury:* Everyman's Library	o	1	o
THOMAS CARLYLE, *French Revolution* (2), *Cromwell* (3), *Sartor Resartus and Heroes and Hero-Worship* (1): Everyman's Library (6 vols.)	o	6	o
THOMAS CARLYLE, *Latter-day Pamphlets:* Chapman and Hall's Edition	o	1	o
CHARLES DARWIN, *Origin of Species:* Murray's Edition	o	1	o
CHARLES DARWIN, *Voyage of the Beagle:* Everyman's Library	o	1	o
A.W. Kinglake, *Eothen:* New Universal Library	o	1	o
John Stuart Mill, *Auguste Comte and Positivism:* New Universal Library	o	1	o
John Brown, *Horae Subsecivae:* World's Classics	o	1	o
John Brown, *Rab and His Friends:* Everyman's Library	o	1	o
Sir Arthur Helps, *Friends in Council:* New Universal Library	o	1	o

Mark Pattison, *Life of Milton:* English Men of Letters Series	0	1	0
F.W. Robertson, *On Religion and Life:* Everyman's Library	0	1	0
Benjamin Jowett, *Interpretation of Scripture:* Routledge's London Library	0	2	6
George Henry Lewes, *Principles of Success in Literature:* Scott Library	0	1	0
Alexander Bain, *Mind and Body*	0	4	0
James Anthony Froude, *Dissolution of the Monasteries,* etc.: New Universal Library	0	1	0
Mary Wollstonecraft, *Vindication of the Rights of Women:* Scott Library	0	1	0
John Tyndall, *Glaciers of the Alps:* Everyman's Library	0	1	0
Sir Henry Maine, *Ancient Law:* New Universal Library	0	1	0
JOHN RUSKIN, *Seven Lamps* (1), *Sesame and Lilies* (1), *Stones of Venice* (3): George Allen's Cheap Edition (5 vols.)	0	5	0
HERBERT SPENCER, *First Principles* (2 vols.)	0	2	0
HERBERT SPENCER, *Education*	0	1	0
Sir Richard Burton, *Narrative of a Pilgrimage to Mecca:* Bohn's Edition (2 vols.)	0	7	0
J.S. Speke, *Sources of the Nile:* Everyman's Library	0	1	0
Thomas Henry Huxley, Essays: Everyman's Library	0	1	0
E.A. Freeman, Europe: Macmillan's Primers	0	1	0
WILLIAM STUBBS, Early Plantagenets	0	2	0
Walter Bagehot, *Lombard Street*	0	3	6

	L	s.	d.
Richard Holt Hutton, *Cardinal Newman*	0	3	6
Sir John Seeley, *Ecce Homo:* New Universal Library	0	1	0
David Masson, *Thomas de Quincey:* English Men of Letters Series	0	1	0
John Richard Green, *Short History of the English People*	0	8	6
Sir Leslie Stephen, *Pope:* English Men of Letters Series	0	1	0
Lord Acton, *On the Study of History*	0	2	6
Mandell Creighton, *The Age of Elizabeth*	0	2	6
F.W.H. Myers, *Wordsworth:* English Men of Letters Series	0	1	0
	L 4	10	6

The following authors are omitted, I think justifiably:— Hallam, Whewell, Grote, Faraday, Herschell, Hamilton, John Wilson, Richard Owen, Stirling Maxwell, Buckle, Oscar Wilde, P.G. Hamerton, F.D. Maurice, Henry Sidgwick, and Richard Jebb.

Lastly, here is the list of poets. In the matter of price per volume it is the most expensive of all the lists. This is due to the fact that it contains a larger proportion of copyright works. Where I do not specify the edition of a book, the original copyright edition is meant:

POETS.	L	s.	d..
WILLIAM WORDSWORTH, *Poetical Works:* Oxford Edition	0	3	6
WILLIAM WORDSWORTH, *Literary Criticism:* Nowell Smith's Edition	0	2	6
Robert Southey, *Poems:* Canterbury Poets	0	1	0

Robert Southey, *Life of Nelson:* Everyman's Library	0	1	0
S.T. COLERIDGE, *Poetical Works:* Newnes's Thin Paper Classics	0	2	0
S.T. COLERIDGE, *Biographia Literaria:* Everyman's Library	0	1	0
S.T. COLERIDGE, *Lectures on Shakspere:* Everyman's Library	0	1	0
JOHN KEATS, *Poetical Works:* Oxford Edition	0	3	6
PERCY BYSSHE SHELLEY, Poetical Works: Oxford Edition	0	3	6
LORD BYRON, *Poems:* E. Hartley Coleridge's Edition	0	6	0
LORD BYRON, *Letters:* Scott Library	0	1	0
Thomas Hood, *Poems:* World's Classics	0	1	0
James and Horace Smith, *Rejected Addresses:* New Universal Library	0	1	0
John Keble, *The Christian Year:* Canterbury Poets	0	1	0
George Darley, *Poems:* Muses' Library	0	1	0
T.L. Beddoes, *Poems:* Muses' Library	0	1	0
Thomas Moore, *Selected Poems:* Canterbury Poets	0	1	0
James Clarence Mangan, *Poems:* D.J. O'Donoghue's Edition	0	3	6
W. Mackworth Praed, *Poems:* Canterbury Poets	0	1	0
R.S. Hawker, *Cornish Ballads:* C.E. Byles's Edition	0	5	0
Edward FitzGerald, *Omar Khayyam:* Golden Treasury Series	0	2	6
P.J. Bailey, *Festus:* Routledge's Edition	0	3	6

Arthur Hugh Clough, *Poems:* Muses' Library	0	1	0
LORD TENNYSON, *Poetical Works:* Globe Edition	0	3	6
ROBERT BROWNING, *Poetical Works:* World's Classics (2 vols.)	0	2	0
Elizabeth Browning, *Aurora Leigh:* Temple Classics	0	1	6
Elizabeth Browning, *Shorter Poems:* Canterbury Poets	0	1	0
P.B. Marston, *Song-tide:* Canterbury Poets	0	1	0
Aubrey de Vere, *Legends of St. Patrick:* Cassell's National Library	0	0	6
MATTHEW ARNOLD, *Poems:* Golden Treasury Series	0	2	6
MATTHEW ARNOLD, *Essays:* Everyman's Library	0	1	0
Coventry Patmore, *Poems:* Muses' Library	0	1	0
Sydney Dobell, *Poems:* Canterbury Poets	0	1	0
Eric Mackay, *Love-letters of a Violinist:* Canterbury Poets	0	1	0
T.E. Brown, *Poems*	0	7	6
C.S. Calverley, *Verses and Translations*	0	1	6
D.G. ROSSETTI, *Poetical Works*	0	3	6
Christina Rossetti, *Selected Poems:* Golden Treasury Series	0	2	6
James Thomson, *City of Dreadful Night*	0	3	6
Jean Ingelow, *Poems:* Red Letter Library	0	1	6
William Morris, *The Earthly Paradise*	0	6	0
William Morris, *Early Romances:* Everyman's Library	0	1	0
Augusta Webster, *Selected Poems*	0	4	6

W.E. Henley, *Poetical Works*	0	6	0
Francis Thompson, *Selected Poems*	0	5	0
	L 5	7	0

Poets whom I have omitted after hesitation are: Ebenezer Elliott, Thomas Woolner, William Barnes, Gerald Massey, and Charles Jeremiah Wells. On the other hand, I have had no hesitation about omitting David Moir, Felicia Hemans, Aytoun, Sir Edwin Arnold, and Sir Lewis Morris. I have included John Keble in deference to much enlightened opinion, but against my inclination. There are two names in the list which may be somewhat unfamiliar to many readers. James Clarence Mangan is the author of *My Dark Rosaleen,* an acknowledged masterpiece, which every library must contain. T.E. Brown is a great poet, recognised as such by a few hundred people, and assuredly destined to a far wider fame. I have included FitzGerald because *Omar Khayyam* is much less a translation than an original work.

SUMMARY OF THE NINETEENTH CENTURY.

83 prose-writers, in 141 volumes, costing L	9	10	7
38 poets " 46 " "	5	7	0
121 187 L	14	17	7

GRAND SUMMARY OF COMPLETE LIBRARY.

	Authors.	Volumes.	Price.
1. To Dryden	48	72	5 9 0
2. Eighteenth Century	57	78	6 8 0
3. Nineteenth Century	121	187	14 17 7
	226	337	L 26 14 7

I think it will be agreed that the total cost of this library is surprisingly small. By laying out the sum of sixpence a day for three years you may become the possessor of a collection of books which, for range and completeness in all branches of literature, will bear comparison with libraries far more imposing, more numerous, and more expensive.

I have mentioned the question of discount. The discount which you will obtain (even from a bookseller in a small town) will be more than sufficient to pay for Chambers's *Cyclopaedia of English Literature,* three volumes, price 30s. net. This work is indispensable to a bookman. Personally, I owe it much.

When you have read, wholly or in part, a majority of these three hundred and thirty-five volumes, *with enjoyment,* you may begin to whisper to yourself that your literary taste is formed; and you may pronounce judgment on modern works which come before the bar of your opinion in the calm assurance that, though to err is human, you do at any rate know what you are talking about.

14

MENTAL STOCKTAKING

Great books do not spring from something accidental in the great men who wrote them. They are the effluence of their very core, the expression of the life itself of the authors. And literature cannot be said to have served its true purpose until it has been translated into the actual life of him who reads. It does not succeed until it becomes the vehicle of the vital. Progress is the gradual result of the unending battle between human reason and human instinct, in which the former slowly but surely wins. The most powerful engine in this battle is literature. It is the vast reservoir of true ideas and high emotions—and life is constituted of ideas and emotions. In a world deprived of literature, the intellectual and emotional activity of all but a few exceptionally gifted men would quickly sink and retract to a narrow circle. The broad, the noble, the generous would tend to disappear for want of accessible storage. And life would be correspondingly degraded, because the fallacious idea and the petty emotion would never feel the upward pull of the ideas and emotions of genius. Only by conceiving a society without literature can it be clearly realised that the function of literature is to raise the plain towards the top level of the peaks. Literature exists so that where one man has lived finely ten thousand may afterwards live finely. It is a means of life; it concerns the living essence.

Of course, literature has a minor function, that of passing the time in an agreeable and harmless fashion, by giving momentary faint pleasure. Vast multitudes of people (among whom may be numbered not a few habitual readers) utilise only this minor function of literature; by implication they class it with golf, bridge, or soporifics. Literary genius, however, had no intention of competing with these devices for fleeting the empty hours; and all such use of literature may be left out of account.

You, O serious student of many volumes, believe that you have a sincere passion for reading. You hold literature in honour, and your last wish would be to debase it to a paltry end. You are not of those who read because the clock has just struck nine and one can't go to bed till eleven. You are animated by a real desire to get out of literature all that literature will give. And in that aim you keep on reading, year after year, and the grey hairs come. But amid all this steady tapping of the reservoir, do you ever take stock of what you have acquired? Do you ever pause to make a valuation, in terms of your own life, of that which you are daily absorbing, or imagine you are absorbing? Do you ever satisfy yourself by proof that you are absorbing anything at all, that the living waters, instead of vitalising you, are not running off you as though you were a duck in a storm? Because, if you omit this mere business precaution, it may well be that you, too, without knowing it, are little by little joining the triflers who read only because eternity is so long. It may well be that even your alleged sacred passion is, after all, simply a sort of drug-habit. The suggestion disturbs and worries you. You dismiss it impatiently; but it returns.

How (you ask, unwillingly) can a man perform a mental stocktaking? How can he put a value on what he gets from books? How can he effectively test, in cold blood, whether he is receiving from literature all that literature has to give him?

The test is not so vague, nor so difficult, as might appear.

If a man is not thrilled by intimate contact with nature: with the sun, with the earth, which is his origin and the arouser of his acutest emotions—

If he is not troubled by the sight of beauty in many forms—

If he is devoid of curiosity concerning his fellow-men and his fellow-animals—

If he does not have glimpses of the nuity of all things in an orderly progress—

If he is chronically "querulous, dejected, and envious"—

If he is pessimistic—

If he is of those who talk about "this age of shams," "this age without ideals," "this hysterical age," and this heaven-knows-what-age—

Then that man, though he reads undisputed classics for twenty hours a day, though he has a memory of steel, though he rivals Porson in scholarship and Sainte Beuve in judgment, is not receiving from literature what literature has to give. Indeed, he is chiefly wasting his time. Unless he can read differently, it were better for him if he sold all his books, gave to the poor, and played croquet. He fails because he has not assimilated into his existence the vital essences which genius put into the books that have merely passed before his eyes;

because genius has offered him faith, courage, vision, noble passion, curiosity, love, a thirst for beauty, and he has not taken the gift; because genius has offered him the chance of living fully, and he is only half alive, for it is only in the stress of fine ideas and emotions that a man may be truly said to live. This is not a moral invention, but a simple fact, which will be attested by all who know what that stress is.

What! You talk learnedly about Shakespeare's sonnets! Have you heard Shakespeare's terrific shout:

> *Full many a glorious morning have I seen*
> *Flatter the mountain-tops with sovereign eye,*
> *Kissing with golden face the meadows green,*
> *Gilding pale streams with heavenly alchemy.*

And yet, can you see the sun over the viaduct at Loughborough Junction of a morning, and catch its rays in the Thames off Dewar's whisky monument, and not shake with the joy of life? If so, you and Shakespeare are not yet in communication. What! You pride yourself on your beautiful edition of Casaubon's translation of *Marcus Aurelius,* and you savour the cadences of the famous:

> This day I shall have to do with an idle, curious man, with an unthankful man, a railer, a crafty, false, or an envious man. All these ill qualities have happened unto him, through ignorance of that which is truly good and truly bad. But I that understand the nature of that which is good, that it only is to be desired, and of that which is bad, that it only is truly odious and shameful: who know, moreover, that this transgressor, whosoever he be, is my kinsman, not by the same blood and seed, but by participation of the same reason and of the same divine particle—how can I be hurt?...

And with these cadences in your ears you go and quarrel with a cabman!

You would be ashamed of your literary self to be caught in ignorance of Whitman, who wrote:

> Now understand me well—it is provided in the essence of things that from any fruition of success, no matter what, shall come forth something to make a greater struggle necessary.

And yet, having achieved a motor-car, you lose your temper when it breaks down half-way up a hill!

You know your Wordsworth, who has been trying to teach you about:

> *The Upholder of the tranquil soul*
> *That tolerates the indignities of Time*
> *And, from the centre of Eternity*
> *All finite motions over-ruling, lives*
> *In glory immutable.*

But you are capable of being seriously unhappy when your suburban train selects a tunnel for its repose!

And the A.V. of the Bible, which you now read, not as your forefathers read it, but with an aesthetic delight, especially in the Apocrypha! You remember:

> Whatsoever is brought upon thee, take cheerfully, and be patient when thou art changed to a low estate. For gold is tried in the fire and acceptable men in the furnace of adversity.

And yet you are ready to lie down and die because a woman has scorned you! Go to!

You think some of my instances approach the ludicrous? They do. They are meant to do so. But they are no more ludicrous than life itself. And they illustrate in the most workaday fashion how you can test whether your literature fulfils its function of informing and transforming your existence.

I say that if daily events and scenes do not constantly recall and utilise the ideas and emotions contained in the books which you have read or are reading; if the memory of these books does not quicken the perception of beauty, wherever you happen to be, does not help you to correlate the particular trifle with the universal, does not smooth out irritation and give dignity to sorrow—then you are, consciously or not, unworthy of your high vocation as a bookman. You may say that I am preaching a sermon. The fact is, I am. My mood is a severely moral mood. For when I reflect upon the difference between what books have to offer and what even relatively earnest readers take the trouble to accept from them, I am appalled (or should be appalled, did I not know that the world is moving) by the sheer inefficiency, the bland, complacent failure of the earnest reader. I am like yourself, the spectacle of inefficiency rouses my holy ire.

Before you begin upon another masterpiece, set out in a row the masterpieces which you are proud of having read during the past year. Take the first on the list, that book which you perused in all the zeal of your New Year resolutions for systematic study. Examine the compartments of your mind. Search for the ideas and emotions which you have garnered from that book. Think, and recollect when last something from that book recurred to your memory apropos of your own daily commerce with humanity. Is it history—when did it throw a light for you on modern politics? Is it science—when did it show you order in apparent disorder, and help you to put two and two together into an inseparable four? Is it ethics—when did it influence your conduct in a twopenny-halfpenny affair between man and man? Is it a novel—when did it help you to "understand all and forgive all"? Is it poetry—when was it a magnifying glass to disclose beauty to you, or a fire to warm your cooling faith? If you can answer these questions satisfactorily, your stocktaking as regards the fruit of your traffic with that book may be reckoned satisfactory. If you cannot answer them satisfactorily, then either you chose the book badly or your impression that you *read* it is a mistaken one.

When the result of this stocktaking forces you to the conclusion that your riches are not so vast as you thought them to be, it is necessary to look about for the causes of the misfortune. The causes may be several. You may have been reading worthless books. This, however, I should say at once, is extremely unlikely. Habitual and confirmed readers, unless they happen to be reviewers, seldom read worthless books. In the first place, they are so busy with books of proved value that they have only a small margin of leisure left for very modern works, and generally, before they can catch up with the age, Time or the critic has definitely threshed for them the wheat from the chaff. No! Mediocrity has not much chance of hood-winking the serious student.

It is less improbable that the serious student has been choosing his books badly. He may do this in two ways—absolutely and relatively. Every reader of long standing has been through the singular experience of suddenly *seeing* a book with which his eyes have been familiar for years. He reads a book with a reputation and thinks: "Yes, this is a good book. This book gives me pleasure." And then after an interval, perhaps after half a lifetime, something mysterious happens to his mental sight. He picks up the book again, and sees a new and profound significance in every sentence, and he says: "I was perfectly blind to this book before." Yet he is no cleverer than he used to be. Only something has happened to him. Let a gold watch be discovered by a supposititious man who has never heard of watches. He has a sense of beauty. He admires the watch, and takes pleasure in it. He says: "This is a beautiful piece of bric-a-brac; I fully appreciate this delightful trinket." Then imagine his feelings when someone comes along with the key; imagine the light flooding his brain. Similar incidents occur in the eventful life of the constant reader. He has no key, and never suspects that there exists such a thing as a key. That is what I call a choice absolutely bad.

The choice is relatively bad when, spreading over a number of books, it pursues no order, and thus results in a muddle of faint impressions each blurring the rest. Books must be allowed to help one another; they must be skilfully called in to each other's aid. And that this may be accomplished some guiding principle is necessary. "And what," you demand, "should that guiding principle be?" How do I know? Nobody, fortunately, can make your principles for you. You have to make them for yourself. But I will venture upon this general observation: that in the mental world what counts is not numbers but co-ordination. As regards facts and ideas, the great mistake made by the average well-intentioned reader is that he is content with the names of things instead of occupying himself with the causes of things. He seeks answers to the question What? instead of to the question Why? He studies history, and never guesses that all history is caused by the facts of geography. He is a botanical expert, and can take you to where the *Sibthorpia europaea* grows, and never troubles to wonder what the earth would be without its cloak of plants. He wanders forth of starlit evenings and will name you with unction all the constellations from Andromeda to the Scorpion; but if you ask him why Venus can never be seen at midnight, he will tell you that he has not bothered with the scientific details. He has not learned that names are nothing, and the satisfaction of the lust of the eye a trifle compared to the imaginative vision of which scientific "details" are the indispensable basis.

Most reading, I am convinced, is unphilosophical; that is to say, it lacks the element which more than anything else quickens the poetry of life. Unless and until a man has formed a scheme of knowledge, be it a mere skeleton, his reading must necessarily be unphilosophical. He must have attained to some notion of the inter-relations of the various branches of knowledge before he can properly comprehend the branch in which he specialises. If he has not drawn an outline map upon which he can fill in whatever knowledge comes to him, as it comes, and on which he can trace the affinity of every part with every other part, he is assuredly frittering away a large percentage of his efforts. There are certain philosophical works which, once they are mastered, seem to have performed an operation for cataract, so that he who was blind, having read them, henceforward sees cause and effect working in and out everywhere. To use another figure, they leave stamped on the brain a chart of the entire province of knowledge.

Such a work is Spencer's *First Principles*. I know that it is nearly useless to advise people to read *First Principles*. They are intimidated by the sound of it; and it costs as much as a dress-circle seat at the theatre. But if they would, what brilliant stocktakings there might be in a few years! Why, if they would only read such detached essays as that on "Manners and Fashion," or "The Genesis of Science" (in a sixpenny volume of Spencer's *Essays*, published by Watts and Co.), the magic illumination, the necessary power of "synthetising" things, might be vouch-safed to them. In any case, the lack of some such disciplinary, co-ordinating measure will amply explain many disastrous stocktakings. The manner in which one single ray of light, one single precious hint, will clarify and energise the whole mental life of him who receives it, is among the most wonderful and heavenly of intellectual phenomena. Some men search for that light and never find it. But most men never search for it.

The superlative cause of disastrous stocktakings remains, and it is much more simple than the one with which I have just dealt. It consists in the absence of meditation. People read, and read, and read, blandly unconscious of their effrontery in assuming that they can assimilate without any further effort the vital essence which the author has breathed into them. They cannot. And the proof that they do not is shown all the time in their lives. I say that if a man does not spend at least as much time in actively and definitely thinking about what he has read as he has spent in reading, he is simply insulting his author. If he does not submit himself to intellectual and emotional fatigue in classifying the communicated ideas, and in emphasising on his spirit the imprint of the communicated emotions— then reading with him is a pleasant pastime and nothing else. This is a distressing fact. But it is a fact. It is distressing, for the reason that meditation is not a popular exercise. If a friend asks you what you did last night, you may answer, "I was reading," and he will be impressed and you will be proud. But if you answer, "I was meditating," he will have a tendency to smile and you will have a tendency to blush. I know this. I feel it myself. (I cannot offer any explanation.) But it does not shake my conviction that the absence of meditation is the main origin of disappointing stocktakings.

✺

BY THE SAME AUTHOR

Novels

A MAN FROM THE NORTH

ANNA OF THE FIVE TOWNS

LEONORA

A GREAT MAN

SACRED AND PROFANE LOVE

WHOM GOD HATH JOINED

BURIED ALIVE

THE OLD WIVES' TALE

THE GLIMPSE

HELEN WITH THE HIGH HAND

CLAYHANGER

THE CARD

Fantasias

THE GRAND BABYLON HOTEL

THE GATES OF WRATH

TERESA OF WATLING STREET

THE LOOT OF CITIES

HUGO

THE GHOST

THE CITY OF PLEASURE

Short Stories

TALES OF THE FIVE TOWNS

THE GRIM SMILE OF THE FIVE TOWNS

Belles-Lettres

JOURNALISM FOR WOMEN

FAME AND FICTION

HOW TO BECOME AN AUTHOR

THE TRUTH ABOUT AN AUTHOR

THE REASONABLE LIFE

HOW TO LIVE ON TWENTY-FOUR HOURS A DAY

THE HUMAN MACHINE

LITERARY TASTE

MENTAL EFFICIENCY

Drama

POLITE FARCES

CUPID AND COMMONSENSE

WHAT THE PUBLIC WANTS

(In Collaboration With Eden Phillpotts)

THE SINEWS OF WAR: A ROMANCE

THE STATUE: A ROMANCE

ooooooooooooooo

business
sociology
lit crit
Fiction 19th C

CPSIA information can be obtained at www.ICGtesting.com
Printed in the USA
LVOW12s1719050215

425868LV00001B/7/P

9 781604 503463